Decision Making

Harvard Business Essentials

The New Manager's Guide and Mentor

The Harvard Business Essentials series is designed to provide comprehensive advice, personal coaching, background information, and guidance on the most relevant topics in business. Drawing on rich content from Harvard Business School Publishing and other sources, these concise guides are carefully crafted to provide a highly practical resource for readers with all levels of experience, and will prove especially valuable for the new manager. To assure quality and accuracy, each volume is closely reviewed by a specialized content adviser from a world-class business school. Whether you are a new manager seeking to expand your skills or a seasoned professional looking to broaden your knowledge base, these solution-oriented books put reliable answers at your fingertips.

Other books in the series:

Finance for Managers
Hiring and Keeping the Best People
Managing Change and Transition
Negotiation
Business Communication
Managing Projects Large and Small
Manager's Toolkit
Crisis Management
Entrepreneur's Toolkit
Time Management
Power, Influence, and Persuasion
Strategy

Decision Making

5 Steps to Better Results

Harvard Business School Press | *Boston, Massachusetts*

978-1-59139-761-8 (ISBN 13)

Library of Congress Cataloging-in-Publication Data
Harvard business essentials : decision making : 5 steps to better results.
p. cm. — (Harvard business essentials series)
Includes bibliographical references.
ISBN 1-59139-761-8
1. Decision making. I. Harvard Business School. II. Series.
HD30.23.H3687 2005
658.4'03—dc22
2005027760

Contents

Decision
Making

Introduction

Decisions. In many respects a business is a series of decisions linked by implementation and other activities. Decisions set the pace and direction; the rest is follow-through.

Given the primacy of decisions, a company can compete and succeed only if it consistently makes good decisions—or, at least, better decisions than its rivals. Apple Computer's decision to take a flier on a digital music file-storage device—the iPod—was a wise decision. That decision, and the implementation work associated with it, revived the company's fortunes and rocketed its stock into the stratosphere.

It naturally follows that bad decisions, especially those made at the top, are costly. Consider the case of Walt Disney Company's 1995 hiring of Michael Ovitz to be its president. Within a year, Disney regretted its choice and ended Ovitz's employment, with a severance package that cost $140 million. That's a lot to pay for a bad decision. But more pain was yet to come. A group of shareholders sued the Disney board for giving away a pile of their money to an employee whose work the board judged to be subpar. That suit, still in progress at this writing, has hit the company with more millions in legal costs and has embroiled its top people and directors in depositions and courtroom appearances. The organization has gotten a black eye over the mess.

But $140 million is small change compared with the losses that companies incur when decision makers make bad merger and acquisition deals. The 2002 merger between Hewlett-Packard and

Compaq cost HP shareholders $24 billion in stock, about 37 percent of the company's total assets. Two years after the costly deal, HP share prices were lagging the S&P 500 (while rival Dell was flourishing), and the company had achieved none of the promised margin improvement in its computer-making operation.

Business leaders often make bad decisions because they do not have all the information they need and because the future is full of surprises. Hindsight makes judgments about past choices easy, but decision makers don't have the benefit of hindsight. They often find themselves flying in the dark, guided only by incomplete data, the council of peers and "experts," and their own intuition.

How good are the decisions made at your company? Chances are they have been less than perfect. That's to be expected because perfection is not possible. Still, you and your colleagues can get closer to it if you have a sound methodology for making decisions and some awareness of common decision traps. This book aims to provide you with both.

Harvard Business Essentials: Decision Making presents a logical, time-tested decision process—one that you can apply to almost any complex situation. The process includes tools you can use to evaluate various alternatives that will help you in reaching your goals. It will also raise your awareness of individual and organizational foibles that cause smart people to make bad choices. And finally, it will tell you how you can make effective decision making a habit within your organization.

As an "essentials" book, this one does not cover all the theory and methodology that scholars have contributed to the field of decision making over the years. Doing that would require many volumes. Instead, its aim is more practical and immediate: to help you make a good start whenever you face an important decision. Whether you are considering the purchase of another business, replacement of your IT system, buying or leasing equipment, or hiring your successor, the process and concepts in this book will show you how to approach the problem—and how to avoid making a bad choice.

What's Ahead

Like other important business activities that aim to convert inputs to outputs, decision making should be addressed as a process. Doing so makes it possible to instruct participants in process steps, to ensure uniform quality, and to improve the quality of your decisions through learning and experimentation. Chapter 1 presents a brief overview of a five-step decision process. Chapter 2 examines the first of those steps: creating a context for success. It is difficult to make good decisions in organizations afflicted by factionalism and a habit of advocacy.

The next process step is to frame the issue properly. Chapter 3 explains how our assumptions, goals, experiences, and expectations can influence how we frame a problem or issue and offers tips on preventing them from blocking a true perception of the problem.

Chapter 4 is about seeking alternatives. Good decisions depend on alternative choices. Here you will learn the characteristics of good alternatives and a method for generating them. The next step is to evaluate each one objectively. Chapter 5 describes tools you can use for that purpose: net present value, a prioritization matrix, a trade-off table, and the decision tree. It also describes several types of computer software you can enlist for the task of alternative evaluation.

At this point in the process, you must make a choice. Even with evaluations of all the alternatives in hand, that choice isn't always easy—particularly when the decision is in the hands of a group. Chapter 6 offers three techniques for moving a group toward agreement on a decision and explains the first step of implementation that should follow.

The remaining chapters consider the broader issues that impact decision quality. Chapter 7 tackles the thorny problem of uncertainty. Decisions are about the future, for which there are no facts; the information we routinely use in reaching decisions is often incomplete. This chapter offers a three-step approach to dealing with uncertainty and describes several tactics you can use to minimize its effects. It also discusses how you can use your intuition in making serious choices clouded in uncertainty.

Uncertainty isn't the only hazard faced by decision makers. They must also contend with their own foibles—behaviors and mental habits that often result in bad choices. These include anchoring, overconfidence, false analogies, and a bias toward evidence that confirms one's own opinions. Chapter 8 takes up these foibles and offers tips on countering them. Chapter 9 follows with a discussion of social and organizational habits that produce the same damaging effects.

The book's final chapter explains the things you can do to make your organization better at making decisions—and at all levels. These include training, practice, and the application of continuous improvement.

Appendix A contains useful implementation tools, including a checklist designed to get your decision off to a good start. Appendix B explains the details of a number of financial tools you can use in evaluating alternatives, including a downloadable interactive tool for conducting breakeven analysis. That tool, and others used in the Harvard Business Essentials series, are available at www.elearning.hbsp .org/businesstools.

The book's endmatter also contains a handy glossary of terms uniquely related to decision making. Whenever you see an italicized word in the text, that's your cue that its definition is listed in the glossary.

Finally, we've included a section titled "For Further Reading." Here you'll find readily available books and articles that can tell you more about the topics covered in this book.

The content of *Decision Making* draws heavily on a number of books, articles, and online publications of Harvard Business School Publishing—in particular, the Making Business Decisions module of Harvard ManageMentor®, an online service. All other sources are noted with standard endnote citations. A number of individuals also contributed information or examples used in the text—in particular, David Matheson, George Labovitz, and Kim Wallace. Many thanks to them.

1

The Decision Process

Five Key Steps

Key Topics Covered in This Chapter

- *Decision making as a process*

- *Five process steps to good decisions*

A S A MANAGER, YOU make decisions every day. Some are straightforward, such as determining which of your subordinates should be assigned to a particular project. Others are complex, such as selecting a new supplier. Consider these two examples:

> *The finance department is moving into new quarters, and Samantha, the department head, needs someone to represent finance on a companywide space-allocation team. For Samantha, this is a straightforward delegation decision: which of her subordinates will be most effective in representing her department? That person must be assertive, must know how to work effectively with others, and must understand the space requirements of the finance department. Samantha knows her people and their capabilities very well. She also knows who can take on added responsibility. So tapping George for the job is an easy decision, and he is eager to accept the assignment. There will be consequences, of course. George will have less time to carry out his regular duties, but neither he nor his manager sees this as a major problem.*

Not all decisions are that easy. Some involve trade-offs, risks, and the interplay of various factors, such as the risk and cost of failure. Consider the following, more complex situation:

> *Precision Interiors (a fictitious name) designs and builds passenger seats and interiors for auto manufacturers in Europe and North America. To remain competitive, it must continually improve its designs and incorpo-*

rate materials that improve passenger comfort and safety within cost and durability constraints. In that spirit, one of its teams has been talking with FiberFuture (another fictitious name), a small supplier that has developed a new material called Zebutek, which resists flames, cushions impact, and absorbs road noise better than all available alternatives. "If we used Zebutek in the interior roof and door linings," speculates one engineer, "it could give us a real advantage. It costs more than the material we're now using, but customers would certainly recognize its value."

The decision to adopt the new material, however, is not simple. There are many trade-offs and risks. The engineer makes the following list:

- *FiberFuture is a small, relatively new company. Will it be capable of delivering the volume of material we need? Can we count on it to deliver on schedule? Will quality be consistent?*

- *What will happen if FiberFuture goes out of business? We'd have to scramble to find a different supplier.*

- *Can our current manufacturing processes work with Zebutek, or will new equipment be needed?*

- *Our customers, the automakers, are struggling to hold the line on costs. Can we pass on the higher cost of this new material to them, or will they resist? Or should we absorb the additional cost and thereby gain market share?*

- *Our current supplier of interior materials has been a reliable and collaborative partner for many years. What will happen to that relationship if 20 to 30 percent of the business is shifted to FiberFuture?*

- *Is there some other supplier on the brink of developing a material that's even better than Zebutek?*

In this second example, Precision Interiors' engineers are faced with a complex and difficult choice—one that makes Samantha's decision seem like a no-brainer. Chances are that you and your colleagues routinely face complex decisions that are this difficult. How do you approach these decisions?

Business decisions are difficult when they involve uncertainty, present many alternatives, are complex, and raise interpersonal issues.

Uncertainty makes us hesitate: "How can I decide when I don't have all the facts, and when I cannot be certain about the outcome of my decision?" Some managers prefer doing nothing to taking what appears to be a leap in the dark.

Alternative courses of action can be equally troubling when each alternative has its own uncertainties and unknowable outcomes. Complexity, too, makes decision making difficult. For example, the acquisition of another firm involves complex legal, accounting, and valuation issues. The transaction is likely to result in substantial layoffs; after all, who needs two accounts receivable departments? But how can you estimate the savings and cost of those layoffs in advance? The acquisition, in turn, is bound to affect your stock price—perhaps for the worse in the short term. Is it really possible to sort out these complex issues?

Decisions also involve interpersonal issues that are difficult to measure and assess but often determine the success or failure of the actions taken.

Over the years, people have developed techniques for dealing with these difficulties, techniques that are part of a logical decision process. This chapter provides an overview of a five-step decision process, as shown in figure 1-1:

1. Establish a context for success.

2. Frame the issue properly.

3. Generate alternatives.

4. Evaluate the alternatives.

5. Choose the alternative that appears best.

Note in figure 1-1 that you begin the entire process by establishing clear objectives (see "High-Quality Output Requires a Good Process"). This point is crucial because the purpose of making decisions is to achieve a meaningful objective.

This chapter takes you on a quick tour of each of the five decision process steps. Later chapters get into the details.

FIGURE 1-1

The decision process

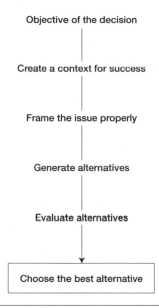

Objective of the decision

Create a context for success

Frame the issue properly

Generate alternatives

Evaluate alternatives

Choose the best alternative

High-Quality Output Requires a Good Process

The notion of a process is basic to decision making. One of the notable discoveries of management thinkers in the past several decades is that process is critical for effective results. Being smart or hardworking does not ensure the quality or quantity of output. It will be haphazard in the absence of an effective process, which is needed whether you're producing ball bearings or automobiles *or making decisions.* When the process is right, quality will improve. If you adopt an effective process and train people in its use, output will improve and will be consistently good. If you continually improve the process, the output will continue to improve.

Step 1: Establish a Context for Success

The first step is to create an environment in which effective decisions are possible. If this task doesn't seem necessary, take a look
around you. If your company is like many others, you'll find that
choices are often influenced by factors that are antithetical to sound
decision making. For example, bickering between individuals elim-
inates rational discussion; management cannot maintain a healthy
level of differences of opinion. A command-and-control culture
tends to make decisions in line with the preferences of powerful individuals. No matter how well informed they may be, in these circumstances every decision is ad hoc, and there is no consistent
approach to dealing with important choices.

A decision-friendly context is generally free of these problems.
In addition, it ensures that the right people participate in the process.
Those people meet in a physical setting that encourages creative
thinking and careful deliberation. A decision-friendly context also
has ground rules that determine how a decision will be made.

Step 2: Frame the Issue Properly

Every successful decision depends on a clear understanding of the
issues at hand and the ways each will affect the objectives of the business. It is critical to determine the nature of the problem. As you'll
see later, you cannot make a good decision if you fail to properly
frame the problem.

Step 3: Generate Alternatives

After the issue has been properly framed, decision makers must develop alternative choices. In the absence of alternatives there can be
no genuine decision.

Step 4: Evaluate the Alternatives

Once you have a realistic set of alternatives, you must assess the feasibility, as well as the risk and implications, of each possible choice.

Many analytical tools—including some software versions—are available for this purpose.

Step 5: Choose the Best Alternative

When all previous steps have been carried out properly and the decision team is in agreement on its objective, the team members can rationally evaluate each of the alternatives. Under ideal circumstances, the right choice will be clear. But in reality, some degree of personal preferences, ambiguity, and dissention often makes the final choice difficult. Fortunately, there are techniques that can help a decision team get through these difficulties. These methods, explained in chapter 6, have fanciful names: catchball, point-counterpoint, and intellectual watchdog. Using these techniques ensures that the merits and demerits of each alternative are fully understood and debated.

It would be easy to believe that mechanically carrying out each of the five process steps will automatically lead to the best possible decision. Unfortunately, this is not the case. Although the five steps can help you organize the decision-making effort, there are many opportunities—sometimes referred to as *decision traps*—for you to make mistakes and allow personal prejudices to channel your thinking. Decision traps are the human biases that cause smart people to make poor choices. We'll address these in chapter 9.

In short, sound decision making is as much an art as a science. It demands good judgment and creativity in addition to technical proficiency.

Summing Up

- Like many other business activities, decision making is more effective, and its quality is more consistent, when it is organized as a process. In the absence of a process, decisions may be ad hoc.

- This book offers a five-step decision process: establish a context for success, frame the issue properly, generate and evaluate alternatives, and choose the best alternative.

2

The Context for Success

Setting the Stage

Key Topics Covered in This Chapter

- *Why context is important for good decisions*

- *The characteristics of a decision-friendly context*

- *The advocacy problem*

- *The inquiry solution*

THE FIVE STEPS OF the decision process are briefly described in chapter 1. Beginning with this chapter, we examine each of those steps in depth, starting with step 1: creating a context for success.

The right context is critical to making successful choices. *Context* refers to the environment of interpersonal relationships and behaviors within which ideas and data are considered and decisions are made. Some organizations and institutions provide environments in which rational dialogue can take place and good decisions can be made. Others are handicapped in this regard. Let's consider three examples of the latter.

Example 1: The U.S. Congress. Making effective decisions in debating forums is as uncommon as harvesting tulips in November. In late 2004, members of the U.S. Congress were faced with the Omnibus Appropriations Bill—a dictionary-length piece of legislation filled with both essential and pork-barrel spending that no one could read or understand in the short time allocated to its discussion and vote. At more than $350 billion, this bill represented a magnitude of spending that exceeded the entire budgets of many countries. It was a year-end catchall bill that threw together every piece of unfinished business. Eager to finish and leave for vacation and the campaigning season, members of Congress passed the bill with little discussion. The results were what one would expect, given the context: undisciplined expenditure of taxpayers' money.

Example 2: A beleaguered manufacturer. In the early 1980s a group of quality assurance managers representing the operating units of a global manufacturer approached the senior executive team. These QA managers had been studying the quality differences between their products and those being made by foreign competitors. The QA group had studied the differences and had assessed their impacts on manufacturing costs, warranty costs, and customer satisfaction. These were compiled in a carefully worded report. "We are alarmed by these findings," said the spokesperson for the QA group as she delivered it.

The CEO and his team thanked the managers for their report and promised to consider it. A week later, and with no dialogue between top management and the QA group, the CEO responded with a memo: "Thanks again for your report. However, I do not agree with its conclusions. Our company defines state-of-the-art manufacturing in this industry. Our products continue to set the standard." Some members of the QA group wondered whether the CEO had even read their report; others wondered whether he had lost touch with what was happening in the industry.

Example 3: Lost in translation. Six employees and a consultant sat around a conference room table. They were there to discuss one of their research and development projects: an attempt to produce a multimedia software program for teaching English to non-English speakers. The project had successfully passed the second of its development milestones and needed renewed approval and continued funding from this review committee before it could move forward. A consultant—an experienced teacher of English as a second language—had been hired to evaluate the program's effectiveness relative to competing products: print, classroom-based, and computer-based. "I'm very impressed with the potential of this program," she told the group. "The program prototype includes all elements needed to make this superior to the best products now on the market." Next to speak was Phil, the project's sponsor. Phil identified the remaining technical challenges and expressed confidence that the development team could overcome them.

The one holdout at the table was Frank, the vice president of finance, who suggested that the project be put on the back burner. "I can't see anything good coming from this project other than cannibalizing the sales of our current products," he said. No one in the room was surprised

by Frank's opposition. Everyone knew that he and Phil were bitter ri-
vals and that Frank had opposed the project from the beginning. Frank
had enormous clout in the company and close ties with the CEO—so
much so that people referred to him as "Little Napoleon." He could—
and did—make life difficult for anyone who crossed swords with him,
and he had the power to frustrate initiatives he did not favor—like this
one. As the discussion continued, everyone but Phil came around to Lit-
tle Napoleon's point of view that the project should be put into neutral.
Even the consultant muted her enthusiasm; she knew where the power
was in this company, and who approved her invoices.

These are only three examples of environments in which effective decision making is an uphill struggle. In the first, elected officials are not willing to take the time to deliberate and weigh the merits of a costly piece of government spending. This is common in political forums where self-interest, antipathy between rival parties, and alliances based on personal benefits dominate the decision-making process. In the case of the manufacturing company, it appears that the key decision maker did not welcome information that contradicted the established view—a sure recipe for disaster. And the R&D project suggests how internal rivalries and the application of personal power discourage the free and open dialogue that underpins effective choice.

Each of these cases illustrates a problem of context. Effective decision making takes place only when the organization and its leaders promote healthy debate and make room for diverse viewpoints. That's why establishing context is step 1 of the decision process.

What, then, are the characteristics of a healthy context? Consider these:

- The right people are asked to participate in decisions.

- Decision makers meet in physical locations that encourage creative thinking.

- Participants agree in advance on how the decision will be made.

- Healthy debate and diverse viewpoints are supported.

  Does your organization have these characteristics?

Get the Right People to Participate

Involving the right people is the first step in creating a context that is conducive to good decisions. The right people are those who are knowledgeable, have experience, and have a stake in the outcome. They include the following:

- **People with the authority to allocate resources and make a decision stick.** One or more persons should have this type of authority. The last thing you want is to spend lots of time hammering out a decision, only to have it ignored or tossed out by senior management. This will demoralize participants and move the organization no closer to a decision.

- **Key stakeholders.** These are the people who will be most directly affected by the decision: those who will be held responsible for results, as well as key implementers of the decision. Because implementers are more likely to support a decision they helped make, including them early in the process will most likely ensure effective follow-through.

- **Experts.** Include experts from inside or outside the organization who have unique knowledge that can be shared with other participants. In most cases these are the people closest to the issue under review. These experts can provide information about the feasibility of various options. For example, if the decision involves replacing certain pieces of manufacturing equipment, a person with firsthand knowledge and experience in that area can help everyone understand the cost of the equipment and its technical merits and demerits. Keep in mind that you may need more than one area of expertise represented in your group.

- **Opponents.** Don't pack the court with cheerleaders for a particular proposal. Instead, invite individuals who might oppose the decision and resist its implementation. If their opposition is well founded, you need to understand their position. It can extend the time needed to reach a desired outcome, but involving potential opponents can reduce resistance down the road.

- **Proponents.** If you involve opponents, it's fitting to include proponents of one or more viewpoints. Just remember that they, like the opponents, will advocate a particular position and cannot be relied on to present a balanced view.

The one thing these disparate individuals should share is commitment to a common goal. They may have different viewpoints and different agendas, but they must be willing to subordinate these to the objective of the company or business unit.

Keep the Size Manageable

Your decision group should be small, preferably no more than six or seven members. Having too few people in the group may leave out individuals who have something important to contribute: the authority to act, resources, expertise, and so forth. Having too many people at the table risks slowing the decision process, particularly when the group includes people who have little to contribute but insist on having a say in the proceedings. A large group also has the effect of silencing people who are not skilled at participating in large group settings. The size of the group may also be dictated by who will be required to implement the final decision.

Use Task Forces As Needed

Depending on the complexity of the decision at hand, you may want to involve more people in the decision-making process. One way to involve many people and yet keep the decision group to a manageable size is to set up task forces to examine certain aspects of the issue.

For example, if you are working on a new e-commerce Web site, you might set up a task force to deal with the technical issues, another composed of representatives from each product line to determine the capabilities of the site, and so forth. The leader of each task force should have a seat at the big table, as illustrated in figure 2-1, where she represents the findings of her task force and any dissenting views. This arrangement has the benefit of harvesting the best

FIGURE 2-1

Task force leaders are members of the decision group

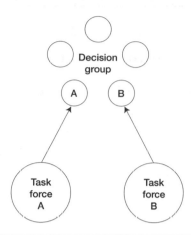

ideas of a great many people while keeping the decision group to a manageable size. It is important to balance the size of the group with the importance or difficulty of implementing a decision.

Give Some Thought to the Setting

To help your group generate creative solutions and evaluate them critically, choose diverse settings for their meetings. Such settings might include conference rooms that you don't typically work in, off-site locations, or a familiar location with the furniture rearranged to facilitate face-to-face discussion. When people are removed from traditional settings, such as a boardroom or a supervisor's office, they tend to speak more freely because they feel less intimidated or constrained by office hierarchies.

Although it many seem superfluous, the arrangement of furniture reveals a great deal about how discussion will take place. If the furniture is set in a circle, there is no obvious "head" or authoritative position. All are equal, and more people are likely to participate in the discussion. If there is an obvious control position, such as at the head of a conference table, the atmosphere will be much the opposite; people will tend to defer to the person who occupies that place.

Agree on How the Decision Will Be Made

Once you've selected the participants and chosen a setting for your meetings, the next step is to determine the decision-making approach you will take. The group you assemble needs to understand up front the process that will be followed and the way the final decision will be made—and by whom.

The spectrum of group decision-making approaches includes the following:

- **Consensus.** All participants meet and discuss the proposal openly. They strive to reach agreement, with everyone accepting the final decision.

- **Qualified consensus.** The decision group attempts to reach a consensus. If it fails to do so, members agree that the official or de facto group leader will make the decision.

- **Majority.** The group votes, and the majority wins. If there is a clear leader of the group, that person might abstain from voting except to break a tie.

- **Directive leadership.** The leader makes the decision and then informs the group of the decision and the reasons that support it. This approach is most effective during times of crisis, when people understand that decisiveness is both appropriate and necessary. The wise leader will assure dissenters that their views are respected and that they were considered: "I appreciate your position, which you have represented very ably. And I have weighed it in my decision. But I respectfully disagree and must pursue another course."

These approaches, with the exception of directive leadership, vary in the extent to which they empower participants and create a sense of responsibility and ownership within the group. Be aware, however, that regardless of the approach, when a group is eager to find agreement it may be tempted to avoid minority viewpoints or areas of conflict. Avoiding contentious areas is a form of self-delusion that often comes back to bite people later (see "The Cost of Conflict Avoidance"). The manager's job is to encourage exploration of all ideas, regardless of the approach you take to making the decision.

The Cost of Conflict Avoidance

The American Civil War (1860–1865) was fought, in part, over slavery, a contentious issue that the country's founders had avoided generations earlier. Pressure by Northern abolitionists—people who were morally and loudly opposed to slavery—was one of the triggers of secession by the slave-owning states of the South. But moral concerns about slavery went back nearly a century and were an important issue in the deliberations that culminated in the U.S. Constitution, signed in 1787. That document is a model of cooperative statesmanship and the art of compromise. But one compromise, an agreement not to press for a resolution to slavery, would come back to haunt the nation.

Squabbling over the slavery question among delegates to the Constitutional Convention was so keen that it threatened to scuttle efforts to draft the Constitution. To avoid that problem, a compromise was reached. Delegates agreed that no constitutional discussion of slavery would take place for at least twenty-five years. This compromise defused the crisis and got everyone off the hook. But it merely put off the day of reckoning. Dissention over slavery grew more intense with the years and eventually split the country. In the end, the grandsons and great-grandsons of the American founders would settle the matter with shot and shell.

From Advocacy to Dialogue

Effective decision making begins with having the right people brought into the process and giving each a proper role. But it goes well beyond that. Some people see their job as advocating for a particular outcome. They mistakenly see the decision process as a contest between their viewpoint and those of others. The process must ensure that advocacy for a particular outcome does not prevail over open-minded inquiry.

Courtroom-like advocacy is common practice in business organizations, but is not conducive to good decisions. Consider the following hypothetical example:

> *Clarissa, the head of product development, is beseeching the CEO to fund development of a new product family. She uses whatever facts, research data, or assumptions support her request. She has also enlisted the help of two powerful executive allies. If Clarissa is aware of contrary data, she will not volunteer it. Meanwhile, Clarissa's opponents are lobbying against her plan, using whatever data support their view.*
>
> *Disappointed with this behavior, the CEO has called a meeting to which he has invited Clarissa's opponents and two other members of the executive team. "Listen," he tells them, "we have limited resources, so we have to determine how best to allocate them. Clarissa has some interesting ideas. Let's discuss them."*
>
> *Clarissa sees this as a cue to make her case. No sooner does she finish her pitch than the discussion spirals into an argument, with her opponents bashing her plan and advocating their own pet projects. The heated conversation goes around in circles, and no decision is made. Everyone leaves the meeting angry and frustrated.*

What went wrong in this example? The CEO did not manage the decision-making process effectively, and the meeting deteriorated into an *advocacy approach*. Clarissa and her detractors approached the meeting as a competition. Each side advocated its position without considering the needs of other departments or the company as a whole. And, like Clarissa, the participants offered only the information that supported their case while omitting details that might weaken it. As a result, the discussion quickly deteriorated into personal attacks.

In a perfect world, this wouldn't happen. The decision about Clarissa's proposal would be made using an *inquiry approach:* an open process in which individuals ask probing questions, explore different points of view, and identify a wide range of options, with the goal of reaching a decision that the group creates and owns collectively. In an inquiry approach, individuals set aside their personal opinions or preferences in order to arrive at a rational decision that is best for the group or organization. They do not advocate on behalf of their pet projects. Table 2-1 compares these two approaches to decision making.

In *The Smart Organization*, David Matheson and Jim Matheson make a clear presentation of the inquiry approach to decision making.[1] The process they describe involves two teams: a decision team (people with the authority to allocate resources) and an investigative

TABLE 2-1

Advocacy versus inquiry

Element	Advocacy	Inquiry
Concept of decision making	A contest	Collaborative problem solving
Purpose of discussion	Persuasion and lobbying	Testing and evaluation
Participants' roles	Spokespeople	Critical thinkers
Patterns of behavior	• Persuade others	• Present balanced arguments
	• Defend your position	• Remain open to alternatives
	• Downplay weaknesses	• Accept constructive criticism
Minority views	Discouraged or dismissed	Cultivated and valued
The outcome	Winners and losers	Collective ownership

Source: David A. Garvin and Michael A. Roberto, "What You Don't Know About Making Decisions," *Harvard Business Review*, September 2001, 110. Reproduced with permission.

team of people with relevant information and experience (the "right people" described earlier in this chapter). Together, these two teams proceed through the steps described in figure 2-2, using dialogue to query, challenge, and gain understanding in order to reach consensus.

As shown in figure 2-2, it's a back-and-forth process, with each step leading toward a decision based on a realistic framing of the problem, an objective analysis, and the development of feasible alternatives. This is similar to the basic decision process laid out in chapter 1. However, the use of two teams—decision makers and investigators—provides an extra level of assurance that inquiry will dominate the natural temptation to advocate.

In the end, the decision team makes the call, but after this back-and-forth method, basing the decision on anything but a rational process would be almost impossible to justify to superiors, peers, and subordinates. (Note: chapter 10 explains how one company, General Motors, has adopted this dialogue decision process and has trained managers and executives in its use.)

FIGURE 2-2

The dialogue decision process

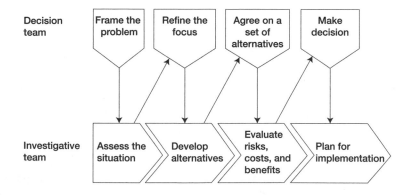

Source: David Matheson and Jim Matheson, *The Smart Organization* (Boston: Harvard Business School Press, 1998), 178. Adapted with permission.

A Hybrid Approach

Although open inquiry is the ideal that all decision forums should seek, some people believe that it is impossible to develop a climate in which people will not argue in favor of their own opinions or personal interests. In their view, a practical and realistic solution to this problem is to seek a balance between advocacy and inquiry.

Using this hybrid approach, group members leave behind their personal agendas and enter the decision forum with the intention of acting as unbiased participants. They may advocate for a position they feel strongly about, but they must also inquire into other viewpoints and consider alternatives. They understand that the goal is to find the best solution for the group as a whole, even if some individuals are negatively affected by the decision. Technical experts and consultants can contribute much to this arrangement. Generally, in well-balanced sessions, people share information freely and consider multiple alternatives.

What is the context for decision making in your company or unit? Is it dysfunctional, based on power and self-serving advocacy, or are decisions made through a rational process of inquiry in which the good of the organization is the primary motivation? Do people agree on how decisions should be made? In the end, contextual factors set the stage for decision making and shape its outcomes. So before anything else is done, you must get the context right.

Appendix A contains a worksheet you can use for setting the stage for future decisions. It asks you to consider doing several things that contribute to the right environment for decision making:

- Describe the objective of the decision.

- List the participants and their roles.

- Determine the time frame within which the decision must be made.

- Identify a physical setting for your meetings.

- Agree on how the decision will be made (consensus, majority rule, etc.).

- Anticipate how you will deal with impasses and advocacy.

Completing each item in this worksheet will force you to think about the decision-making context of your organization and ways you can change it for the better.

Summing Up

- The organizational context for decision making has an impact on how decisions will be made. A healthy context includes the right people, puts them in an appropriate physical setting, ensures that they agree on how decisions will be made, and supports diverse views and healthy debate.

- When a group is making a decision, be sure that it includes people who have the authority to allocate resources and make the decision stick.

- Limit the decision group to six or seven people. If more are needed, assign some of the work to task forces whose leaders are part of the decision group.

- The spectrum of decision-making approaches includes consensus, qualified consensus, majority rule, and directive leadership. The latter is most effective in times of crisis.

- Advocacy is antithetical to effective decision making. Too many businesspeople approach the decision process as a contest that they must try to win. The antidote to advocacy is rational and open-minded inquiry.

3

The Framing Challenge

What Is the Real Problem?

Key Topics Covered in This Chapter

- *Frames as mental windows on reality— for better or worse*

- *How to avoid misframing a problem or decision*

- *Using creative thinking to develop a proper frame*

FRAMING THE PROBLEM IS the second step in the decision process. We've stated elsewhere that a *frame* is a mental window through which we view a particular problem, situation, or opportunity. As Alan Rowe put it, frames are "the prisms through which we view the world . . . they determine both what we see and how we interpret it."[1] So strong are frames that they can channel our thinking even when empirical evidence supports another view.

We all have these mental frames, and they can be extremely useful in helping us navigate through a complex world. Among other things, an appropriate frame helps us avoid solving the wrong problem. If you frame the problem wrong you'll never solve it, but frame it correctly and you're halfway to the solution.

Our particular frame is usually influenced by our assumptions, goals, education, experience, expectations, and prejudices. Consider, for example, three people trying to ship packages from their local post office. One of the customers is a recent immigrant from one of the former Soviet Bloc states, another is the operations manager from a nearby manufacturing plant, and the third is an entrepreneur and founder of three successful companies. Although twenty people are in line at the moment, only two postal employees are available to help them.

Everyone in the slow-moving line is frustrated with the pace of progress except one person: the immigrant. In fact, she is impressed by the service. "Back in the old country," she tells the person behind her, "there would have been only one person working at the counter, and he would take a break every half-hour, leaving everyone to stand in line. It's so much better here."

The operations manager has a much different perspective. "This is a classic bottleneck," he tells himself. "I'm sure that someone could reengineer the entire process to make things move more quickly and at less cost."

Meanwhile, the entrepreneur is pleased by the experience of waiting in line because it has given him something of great potential value: an idea for a new business. "I wonder what people would pay for a no-waiting alternative to the post office—a postal shop with self-service kiosks?" His mind is already churning with ideas about using technology to cut waiting time and make a nice profit for him.

Each of these three individuals observes the post office experience through a different mental frame. This is natural because our experiences and expectations have an impact on how we see things. But when it comes to making a decision, beginning with an inappropriate or erroneous frame can lead you to an ineffective conclusion. Alternatively, you may successfully solve the wrong problem—or solve it in the wrong way!

This chapter discusses the importance of properly framing a problem in terms of the reality of the situation and the objectives of the organization. It explains how an improperly framed problem can shut out feasible alternatives and result in low-quality decisions, and it offers tips for doing it right.

Perils and Promise

In their excellent description of framing, J. Edward Russo and Paul J. H. Schoemaker warn that "when it comes to making decisions, the way people frame a problem—i.e., the particular perspective that they (often unconsciously) adopt—exerts enormous power over the options they will recognize and the solutions they will favor."[2] Thus, the immigrant in our example saw no need for options in handling postal customers. From her perspective, everything was fine. The manager of the post office would probably agree.

In contrast, the operations manager and the entrepreneur were open to options and different solutions precisely because they observed the situation through very different frames. The operations manager, given his work experience, immediately viewed the slow-moving queue as a process problem amenable to improvement. This is reminiscent of the old saying that if you're a hammer, everything looks like a nail.

People who understand framing also understand its power to exert influence. They know that if they can frame the issue or the agenda as they see it, they have a greater chance of producing the decision they favor. As Jeffrey Pfeffer has written in *Managing with Power,* "Establishing the framework within which issues will be viewed and decided is often tantamount to determining the result."[3]

This is not a problem as long as you encourage people to adopt a frame that benefits the organization. Consider this example:

> *A group of publishing executives has convened to discuss a proposal offered by David, one of the company's managers. David has proposed that the company acquire the rights to a ten-volume self-paced learning course that is currently being used to prepare newly hired securities salespeople for the licensing examination. The publication is not like anything the company has previously published, and it will involve direct selling to end customers instead of selling through book wholesalers and retailers, who are given 50 percent discounts from the list price.*
>
> *The senior financial person at the table quizzes David about the projected revenues and costs of manufacturing and distribution. The financial vice president is far from enthusiastic. "Based on your projections, this project would have a positive net present value, but just barely," she says. "And the rate of return is below what we demand of new projects."*
>
> *The marketing executive picks up where the first interrogator leaves off, asking for more details about unit sales prices and David's method for generating his revenue projections.*
>
> *David can see that the meeting is going to be a predictable and negative evaluation of the project if revenues and costs constitute the sole frame of reference. Unless he acts quickly, the novelty of the publi-*

cation for this company, and its potential impact on the company's future growth, will not be considered.

To everyone's surprise, David doesn't respond to the numbers questions. Instead, he politely deflects the first round of questions and launches into something unanticipated. "This proposal isn't about the profits of a single project," he begins. "It's about an opportunity to break out of the rut we've been in for the past ten years by entering a new market—a market with fat profit margins and major growth potential. It's about an opportunity to sell directly to our customers instead of through the wholesalers and national book chains, who take most of the profits out of our work and our products."

The assembled executives are slightly stunned but are now attentive. David has hit two important hot buttons: fat profit margins and major growth. So they give him the floor. "Whether this particular product makes money or loses money is much less important than the publishing opportunities we are likely to find once we gain a beachhead in that new market," David says. He makes an analogy between his project and the Normandy invasion during World War II. "By traditional measures, the first day of the invasion was a costly loss. If people calculated the gains and losses of only that one day, they would have to say, 'We should have stayed in England.' But that single day opened the door to a larger victory."

After a pause, the executives resume their questions. But their queries are no longer about short-term sales and expense projections; instead, they are about how David's project might help the company grow and become more profitable.

In this example, David decisively reframes the discussion in a way that serves his purpose and what he believes to be best for the company. That might be fine for David, but is his framework the right one for approaching the problem? The question is worth asking because inappropriate framing will almost surely lead to a bad decision. The best way to avoid misframing is to follow these guidelines:

- Don't automatically accept an initial framing. Always ask, "Is this the issue? Is this the problem?" The frame may be inappropriate, or someone may be trying to channel your thinking into a particular framework.

- Seek many perspectives on the problem. Before you make any decisions, look at it from different angles. Then talk over the possibilities.

- Attempt to discover the frames used by other people in the decision group, including your own. What biases do they reflect?

- Uncover and challenge whatever assumptions lie beneath the dominant prospective, including your own. This is your best insurance against advocacy by others.

- Put yourself in a different person's shoes as you approach a problem. Decision scholar Alan Rowe refers to this as "opposite think." For example, if you are facing a product design decision, approach it from the perspectives of nonexpert users or repair personnel. When Ford Motor Company was developing its now ubiquitous Taurus model in the 1980s, it took the unprecedented step of asking mechanics from its dealer network to critique its design at different stages. These mechanics, the people who would eventually have to repair the new automobile, had a much different outlook than did the people designing it.

Don't Impose Your Frame on Others

Perhaps the toughest challenge is to avoid the very human urge to assume that your framing is correct and then trying to bring others around to your view. Persuading others is appropriate, but only when you have taken the five precautions just listed.

In the earlier example, David didn't like the frames that others were using to evaluate his proposal. So he pushed back and replaced theirs with his own frame. The danger here, as noted, is that David's frame may be wrong.

Many managers make the mistake of imposing their mental frames on others. In so doing they seek solutions before they understand the nature of the problem. Consider the following example:

A toy manufacturer has a customer support phone line to answer questions about how to assemble its products. The volume of customer calls has increased so much that support personnel cannot keep up with them. Customers have complained of waiting half an hour to get help.

The manager responsible for the support line has put together a team to help him decide on the best way to address the issue. He begins the first meeting by saying, "We have a serious problem with our customer support line. Customers are waiting too long for service. We need to fix it."

By framing the issue as a problem with the phone line response time, the manager has focused the decision team on ways to reduce the response time—for example, adding more phone lines, adding more phone representatives, increasing the hours of service. These solutions will address the symptoms of the problem—overloaded phone lines—but may not address the root cause. To get to the root of the problem, the team should be thinking about *why* customer calls have increased dramatically. Is a specific product responsible for an inordinate number of calls? Is there a flaw in the design of a product, or in the assembly instructions? Are the phone support associates poorly trained?

Suppose the manager had framed the issue by saying, "We have a serious problem with our customer support line. The volume of calls has increased, customers are waiting too long for service, and we need to find out why. Then we need to decide what to do about it." The focus of the team would be quite different.

Apply Creative Thinking

Coming early in the decision-making or problem-solving process, framing is a good place to apply creative thinking. It costs nothing and takes little time, and yet it has the potential of steering the decision process into new and more useful directions.

One approach is to mentally stand outside yourself and consider the decision or problem from an "outside-in" perspective. Detaching yourself from your usual perspective is not easy, but if you can do it you have a chance to see any situation with new eyes. One example of the outside-in perspective is viewing your company—or one of its features—through the eyes of a customer. To do this you can conduct market research, but that is expensive and slow. A quicker, less expensive option is simply to put yourself in the customer's shoes and try to do business with your own company. Ask a trusted friend or family member to do the same.

Start by trying to get information about your company's products or services. How easy or difficult is this? Then make a purchase through the typical distribution channels. What is your experience in making a purchase through the company's toll-free telephone number or Web site? Now try to report a problem to the dealer or the company's customer service department, and note how it is handled.

The aim of this creative approach is to understand your company from the customer's perspective. That understanding will put you in the best possible position to frame problems and make improvements.

When you're confronted with a problem or decision, think about how to frame the issue for your team. Never assume from the outset that you know what the problem is. Instead, challenge yourself and your team to get at the core of the issue by framing the problem in a variety of ways and assessing whether the available information supports your theories. Throughout the process, ask open-ended questions that encourage exploration rather than closed questions based on predefined assumptions about the problem.

Here are examples of open-ended questions that generate discussion and idea sharing:

"What evidence do you have that we have a problem?"

"Is the problem isolated, or does it extend to other units?"

"How can we measure the magnitude of the problem?"

Closed questions, in contrast, usually elicit a yes or no response:

"So, you've talked with those two departments about this?"

"And you are convinced that we need to make a decision quickly?"

Discussion and idea sharing will eventually lead you to a proper framing of the problem. And when you have that, you'll be ready for the next step of the decision process: generating alternatives.

Summing Up

- A frame is a mental window through which we view a problem, situation, or opportunity.

- If you frame the situation incorrectly, you'll probably make a bad decision; if you frame it correctly, you'll be halfway to a good decision.

- Be wary. Some people will try to frame the issue to suit their personal agendas.

- Never accept the initial frame. Actively seek others.

- Look for bias and false assumptions in all frames.

4

Alternatives

The Source of Superior Solutions

Key Topics Covered in This Chapter

- *Why good decisions depend on alternative choices*

- *A method for generating alternatives*

- *How a creative group can help*

- *The characteristics of good alternatives*

GOOD DECISIONS EMERGE from a set of feasible alternatives. Decision makers in these situations don't simply say yes or no to a single choice. Instead, they say, "That's an interesting idea, but it cannot be the only one. Let's think of other options before we do anything else."

> *George, a marketing manager at a consumer products company, calls a meeting of his team to discuss laundry detergent sales in Latin America. "Our sales in Latin America are 23 percent below what we anticipated a year ago, when we first entered that market," he says. "We need to get things moving—and fast. I'm looking for ideas."*
>
> *Everyone waits for someone else to speak. Impatiently, George breaks the silence by suggesting they consider changing the current packaging. "I've noticed that our competitors typically sell their detergent in smaller packages than they do in the States. They may know something we don't about buyer behavior."*
>
> *Following this cue, Kim chimes in with her own reflections about packaging and consumer trends. Another person then describes the packaging of a product that has sold particularly well in Latin America. Everyone seems to have ideas to offer about packaging and how a change there might improve sales. The meeting concludes with the creation of a task force to research new packaging options.*

Is a change in packaging the best solution for this company? Possibly. A task force charged with finding new packaging options might produce something of real value. But given the problem of disappointing Latin American sales, there may be alternative solutions of even greater value—for example, a change in pricing or a different approach to advertising and promotion. Perhaps the product itself should be altered in some tangible way. However, George and his team will never know the merits of these other solutions if they immediately take the packaging route.

Decision makers should always seek alternatives. This chapter explains the value of alternative decision options and presents practical ideas for generating them.

Generating Alternatives

To make an informed decision, you need choices. Alternatives are those choices. After weighing the merits of a variety of alternatives, you will be in a better position to make the best decision for a given situation. In the absence of alternatives, people are faced only with a yes-or-no choice: Should we do this or not? That's not much of a choice, and it rarely produces an effective decision. Decision experts David Matheson and Jim Matheson go even further, stating, "Creative and doable alternatives are preconditions for any decision. If there are no alternatives, there is no decision."[1]

What you want are alternatives that represent a range of possibilities, even if the decision team must actively produce them. How are alternatives generated? Let's return for a moment to the example that opened the chapter. George and his team were talking about how they could increase sales for their detergent product in Latin America. This meeting seemed to proceed smoothly. What, then, went wrong?

In this scenario, the manager did not successfully engage the team in generating alternatives. He didn't promote healthy debate and constructive conflict. Instead, excessive group harmony resulted in a single-minded pursuit of the first idea that emerged: to investigate packaging options. There was little creativity or innovative thinking. As a result, no new ideas surfaced, and the group settled on the first alternative suggested, which had been the manager's idea.

As a decision maker, your goal at this stage is to identify as many alternatives as possible. Brainstorming is an effective way to generate various ideas and courses of action.

Brainstorming

Brainstorming is a technique used to generate alternatives and problem solutions. It can be done by individuals, but it works better in groups because the insights and experiences of many people almost always produce more ideas than a person working alone, no matter how brilliant that person might be.

To brainstorm for alternatives, begin with a blank flipchart page or a clean whiteboard. Ask people to suggest any ideas that come into their heads, or ask individuals to take a few minutes to develop their own lists of ideas to share publicly. Either way, record those ideas, but don't discuss their merits or allow criticism—at least not yet.

If you are leading the session, be scrupulously neutral as you recognize each contribution. Don't do anything that would signal your like or dislike of any of the alternatives presented. For example, avoid statements like these: "Thank you, Jean—that's the best idea we've heard all morning" or "Thanks, Herb. I doubt if that alternative is feasible, but I'll add it to the list." Comments like these can prejudice people for or against ideas even before their merits are discussed. Neutrality is essential when the brainstorming leader has substantial influence over the group.

Brainstorming works best when people feel comfortable in speaking their minds, especially when their ideas conflict with those of their peers or their boss (see "Tips for Generating Alternatives"). The atmosphere must also encourage shy people to participate. We know from experience that there are some people who naturally speak up in group sessions. They tend to be outgoing and assertive, and they can easily dominate the discussion. But being outgoing and assertive doesn't correlate with having superior ideas. The person sitting silently at the far end of the table may have the best idea of the group. If you're leading the session, it's your job to elicit her ideas.

Tips for Generating Alternatives

When you meet to generate alternative choices, follow these tips.

- Invite outsiders, experts as well as novices, to participate periodically in your meetings. Outsiders provide fresh ideas, a different perspective, and meaningful critiques.

- Conduct external benchmarking to observe how other companies and other industries address problems that are similar to yours.

- Encourage decision team members to step out of their traditional roles when generating alternatives. For example, if you're trying to brainstorm new product ideas, invite someone from your marketing group to participate, but ask that person to think about ideas from a financial perspective. You will probably find that more creative ideas surface when people think without their functional hats on.

- Ask probing questions such as, "What alternatives should we consider?" and "How should we respond to concerns about _____?" In this way, you avoid deciding too early on a solution that may not be the best one. Among the most important probing questions are those that test the validity of the group's assumptions. Those assumptions should be made explicit and discussed openly.

- Be willing to consider and discuss views that differ from your own. This is not easy, and the group leader should be the model for this behavior. If the leader demonstrates tolerance for and interest in ideas contrary to her own, others may notice and follow suit.

- Revisit abandoned alternatives from time to time to ensure that they were discarded for sound reasons.

Continued

- Don't overlook *hybrid alternatives*. In many cases it's possible to combine the best features of two or more existing alternatives into a new and superior alternative. For example, the popular sport utility vehicle (SUV) is a hybrid that brings together the best features of a light truck and a regular station wagon. Similarly, the minivans that first appeared in the 1980s combine the most popular features of a boxy, trucklike van with the comforts of a passenger car.

This is one of those situations when it's useful to ask people to write down their ideas and pass them to the session leader. A creative problem-solver who happens to be shy in a group setting may have no trouble articulating her ideas in written form.

Encourage open, candid dialogue by making it clear at the outset that the final outcome is not predetermined and everyone's input will be valued. Suggest that people think outside their individual or departmental roles. They should focus on what is best for the company using all the available information.

When participants have run out of ideas, take a look at the many ideas you've written down on the flip chart. How many are there? If the list contains numerous ideas, it may be possible to group them under common themes. For example, the detergent company team might group its alternatives for boosting sales under these headings: packaging, pricing, retail displays, special promotions, product reformulation. Grouping related ideas helps to focus the effort.

There is some evidence that you can get more out of brainstorming when ideas are generated independently and later brought into a group session in which people can share and build on their ideas.[2] This technique prevents the convergence of ideas—through persuasion or peer pressure—that normally occurs when people with different ideas begin talking to each other. There are plenty of opportunities for discussion and convergence later.

Alternatives provide the choices you will need to make an informed decision. When you encourage team participation, facilitate creative conflict, and listen to ideas, you are likely to generate a full slate of options that will serve you well as you enter the next stage: evaluating alternatives.

Bring a Creative Group to the Task

Your search for alternatives will be more successful if you bring a creative group to the task. Groups can often achieve greater creative output than individuals working alone because they bring a greater sum of competencies, insights, and energy to the effort. But to reap this greater potential, groups must have a diversity of thinking styles and skills. That diversity has several benefits:

- Individual differences can produce a creative friction that sparks new ideas.

- Diversity of thought and perspective are a safeguard against *groupthink,* the tendency of individual thought to converge for social reasons around a particular point of view.

- Diversity of thought and skills will give good ideas more opportunities to develop.

Thus, managers need to consider how work groups are staffed and how they communicate.

A creative group exhibits paradoxical characteristics. It shows tendencies of thought and action that we might assume to be mutually exclusive or contradictory. For example, to do its best work, a group needs deep knowledge of the subjects relevant to the problem it's trying to solve, and a mastery of the processes involved. But at the same time, the group needs fresh perspectives that are not encumbered by the prevailing wisdom or established ways of doing things. Often called a "beginner's mind," this is the perspective of a newcomer: someone who is curious, even playful, and willing to ask anything—no matter how naive the question may seem. Thus, bringing together contradictory characteristics can catalyze new ideas.

Although diversity of thinking and skills is valuable in identifying alternatives, it presents hazards. Different thinking styles do not produce unbroken harmony—nor would you want it to. Expect disagreement. The manager's job is to turn friction into productive thinking. For this to happen people in the group must listen to each other, must be willing to understand different viewpoints, and must question each other's assumptions.

At the same time, managers must prevent conflict from becoming personal or from going underground, where resentment can simmer. The best antidote to destructive conflict is to establish a set of group norms of behavior. What should your group's operating norms be? That depends on the purpose of the group and the personalities of its members. Just be sure that the rules are clear and concise and that people know and agree to observe them. Here are a few examples of group norms:

- Every group member should show respect to others.

- Everyone should make a commitment to active listening.

- Everyone has a right to disagree and an obligation to challenge others' assumptions.

- Everyone will have an opportunity to speak.

- Conflicting views are an important source of learning.

- Ideas and assumptions may be attacked, but individuals may not (see "Three Steps for Handling Creative Conflict").

- Calculated risk taking is good.

- Failures should be acknowledged and examined for their lessons.

- Playful attitudes are welcomed.

- Successes will be celebrated as a group.

Whatever norms your group adopts, make sure that all members have a hand in creating them and that everyone is willing to abide by them.

Three Steps for Handling Creative Conflict

Even when your group has a consensus on its norms of behavior, conflict is a fact of life in groups, even creative groups. But conflict is not inherently bad. In fact, the friction caused by conflict can kindle breakthrough ideas if the conflict is handled well. The following three steps will help you turn conflict into a creative asset.

1. Create a climate that makes people willing to discuss difficult issues. Help your team understand the concept of "the moose on the table": the big issue or problem that is impeding progress but that no one wants to discuss. Make it clear that you *want* the tough issues aired and that *anyone* can point out a moose.

2. Facilitate discussion. How do you deal with a moose after it has been identified? Use the following guidelines:

   • Stop whatever you are doing and acknowledge the issue, even if only one person sees it.

   • Refer to the group norms you have adopted to govern how people treat each other.

   • Encourage the person who identified the moose to be specific.

   • Keep the discussion impersonal. The point is not to assign blame; discuss what, and not who, is impeding progress.

   • If the issue involves someone's behavior, encourage the person who identified the problem to explain how the behavior affects him, rather than make assumptions about the motivation behind the behavior.

3. Move toward closure by discussing what can be done.

   • Leave with concrete suggestions for improvement, if not a solution.

   • If the subject is too sensitive and discussions are going nowhere, consider adjourning your meeting until a specified later date so that people can cool down. Or consider bringing in a facilitator.

Characteristics of Good Alternatives

It's one thing to create a list of alternatives; it's quite another to create good ones. A list of bad alternatives will only put you in the undesirable position of having to choose between two (or more) evils. A list of good ideas produces the opposite effect.

But what, exactly, is a good alternative? As described by David Matheson and Jim Matheson in *The Smart Organization*, good alternatives have these characteristics:

- They are broadly constructed and not simply minor variations of another concept.

- They are genuine alternatives that do not exist solely to make another choice appear superior and reasonable; nor are they warmed-over ideas that have already been rejected for good reasons.

- They are feasible choices in terms of the company's capabilities and resources.

- They are "sufficiently numerous to represent a true choice, yet not so numerous as to confound the ability to evaluate and choose."[3]

Let's consider each of these criteria in more detail.

BROADLY CONSTRUCTED. Many if not most decisions can support a broad spectrum of possible courses of action. In seeking the best distribution strategy, for example, a consumer products company could justifiably entertain many alternatives: brick-and-mortar retail shops (in malls and freestanding stores), catalog sales, online distribution, sales through a number of individual wholesaler arrangements, or a combination of these. Together, these alternatives offer decision makers a broad range of options.

GENUINE. The expression "straw man" indicates a weak argument or alternative. The straw man is put up for one purpose: to make some other alternative look reasonable or strong. The straw man is nothing more than a false choice and should be excluded from any list of decision alternatives.

FEASIBLE. Some ideas are great alternatives for one company but infeasible for others. For example, the idea of building a new 500-passenger transcontinental airliner is a feasible alternative for Airbus or Boeing, but not for Piper Aircraft Company, which lacks the resources to undertake so massive a project. It's always important to think big when you're brainstorming alternatives, but it's equally important to be realistic.

The feasibility of an alternative is ultimately tested through detailed evaluation, a subject we'll get to a bit later. However, evaluation takes time and, often, money. So a decision team should eliminate suggested alternatives that clearly will fail the feasibility test because they are on their face too costly, too ambitious given the scope of the problem, or Band-Aid solutions. As Vincent Barabba aptly put it in his own description of generating alternatives, "Why waste resources examining a course of action that will never be taken?"[4]

SUFFICIENTLY NUMEROUS. You want to create enough alternatives to give decision makers a full range of options without overburdening them with more than they can handle. The notion that "if five alternatives are good, fifty are better" does not hold. Be pragmatic. Always remember that options that make the final list will have to be evaluated, a process that will consume the time and attention of many of your company's more valuable people.

At this point, you might want to think about recent decisions in which you've played a part. Ask yourself, "Did we generate alternatives that met these standards?" That is, were your alternatives broadly constructed, genuine, feasible, and sufficiently numerous to give decision makers a real choice? If they were not, try harder next time, using the ideas provided in this chapter.

Summing Up

- In the absence of alternatives, there is no real decision to be made. As a decision maker, one of your jobs is to identify a manageable set of good alternatives.

- Brainstorming is a useful technique for generating alternatives and problem solutions. But remember that it works only when people feel comfortable in speaking their minds.

- Don't overlook hybrid alternatives, which combine the best features of two or more other alternatives.

- You will have greater success if you enlist people who have diverse skills and viewpoints. This will generate creative conflict. As a manager, your job is to turn this conflict into a productive direction.

- According to experts, good alternatives are broadly constructed, genuine, feasible, and sufficiently numerous to give decision makers a real set of choices.

5

Evaluate the Alternatives

Finding the Value of Each Option

Key Topics Covered in This Chapter

- *Variables to consider in evaluating alternatives*

- *Financial tools for analysis*

- *Ways to use prioritization matrices and trade-off tables*

- *Using a decision tree to see the big picture*

- *Types of decision software*

I N T H E Y E A R S L E A D I N G up to the American Revolution, Benjamin Franklin moved from Philadelphia to London, where he acted as a colonial agent to the British government. His keen intellect and scientific reputation quickly gained him entry to the highest circles of British letters and science. Among his new acquaintances was Joseph Priestley, a self-taught pioneer in the field of chemistry.

Priestley had a problem. He had been offered a post in London with excellent pay and prestige. But taking the offer would require moving from his hometown of Leeds and would interfere with his scientific experiments. What should he do? He turned to his sage friend, Franklin, for advice.

Franklin appreciated Priestley's problem; indeed, he found himself in a similar situation. On the one hand, he relished the lively intellectual atmosphere of London and the friendships he had established among Britain's scientific and cultural elite. On the other hand, he missed Philadelphia, his family, and his old friends. There were reasons to stay in London but also reasons to return to America. How could he choose between them?

Franklin had a method for dealing with this type of decision problem, a method he shared with Priestley by letter in September 1772. Such decisions were difficult, Franklin wrote, because people usually heard all the arguments in favor of one alternative, and then all the arguments against, in a series. They rarely examined the pros and cons as a single piece; that made it difficult to weight the positive and negative aspects of the alternatives. His remedy, as Franklin explained to Priestley, was to place them all together and to mentally assign weights or priorities to each.

> *My way is to divide half a sheet of paper by a line into two columns,*
> *writing over the one Pro, and over the other Con. Then during three*
> *or four days' consideration I put down under the different heads short*
> *hints of the different motives that at different times occur to me for or*
> *against the measure. When I have thus got them all together in one*
> *view, I endeavour to estimate their respective weights, and where I*
> *find two, one on each side, that seem equal, I strike them both out. If*
> *I find a reason pro equal to some two reasons con, I strike out the*
> *three. If I judge some two reasons con equal to some three reasons pro,*
> *I strike out the five; and thus proceeding I find at length where the*
> *balance lies.*[1]

Franklin, a man ahead of his time on many things, was practicing in the eighteenth century something similar to the technique decision theorists today call *even swaps*.[2] He was evaluating alternatives and weighing their respective merits. In this chapter you'll learn several practical techniques for doing the same thing.

Variables to Consider

Once you and your decision team have identified a set of alternatives, you must estimate how well each one meets the objective you established at the outset of the process. How much value does each alternative contribute to the objective?

In answering that question, managers must contend with many variables:

- **Costs.** How much will the alternative cost? Will it result in a cost savings now or over the long term? Are there any hidden costs? Are there likely to be additional costs down the road? Does this alternative fall within the budget?

- **Benefits.** What profits or other benefits will we realize if we implement a given alternative? Will it increase the quality of our product? Will customer satisfaction increase? Will it make our people more effective?

- **Financial impact.** How will the monetary costs and benefits of this choice translate into bottom-line results as measured by net present value? What will be the timing of that result? Will implementation require us to borrow money?

- **Intangibles.** Will our reputation improve if we implement a given alternative? Will our customers or employees be more satisfied and loyal?

- **Time.** How long will it take to implement this alternative? What is the probability of delays and the impact of delays on the schedule?

- **Feasibility.** Can this alternative be implemented realistically? Are there any obstacles that must be overcome? If it is implemented, what resistance might be encountered inside or outside the organization?

- **Resources.** How many people are needed to implement each alternative? Are they available, or will we need to hire and train them? What other projects will suffer if individuals focus on this option?

- **Risk.** What risks are associated with this alternative? For example, could it result in loss of profits or competitive advantage? How might competitors respond? Because risk and uncertainty are essentially the same thing, what information would reduce these uncertainties? Would it be difficult and costly to obtain risk-reducing information?

- **Ethics.** Is this alternative legal? Is it in the best interests of customers, employees, and the community where we operate? Would we feel comfortable if other people knew that we were considering this alternative?

There is little doubt that your decisions must take into account these same considerations. Obviously, some will be more important to your company than others. But one that always ranks high in the pecking order of business concerns is financial impact, as determined by an appropriate financial analysis.

Financial Analysis

When strategic and capital budgeting decisions are at stake, companies put heavy stress on financial measures of value. After all, businesses are interested in alternatives that will create the most financial value for their owners. They focus on the bottom-line impact of various choices.

Financial value is usually expressed as *net present value* (NPV), which is the *present value* (PV) of one or more future cash flows minus any initial investment costs. Present value, in turn, is defined as the monetary value today of a future payment discounted at some annual compound rate.

NPV is among the most powerful and useful decision tools available to managers. Whether you're considering the development of a new product, the purchase of a new asset, or any other type of investment, this tool can greatly enhance your decisions. Best of all, it accounts for your company's cost of capital in those decisions.

In a simplified form, NPV analysis works as follows:

1. Estimate the future annual cash flows of the alternative.

2. Discount each cash flow by some predetermined interest rate (usually your firm's cost of capital—generally in the 10–15 percent range).

3. Add up the discounted cash flows.

4. Subtract the initial cash investment.

For example, let's assume that alternative A is a new $250,000 piece of capital equipment that you might buy and install. Your engineers forecast the associated costs and benefits and calculate that the equipment will produce a positive cash flow of $70,000 per year for five years, as shown in table 5-1; after this, they assume that the equipment will be worn out and without value. On the recommendation of the chief financial officer, you discount these annual cash flows by 10 percent—the company's cost of capital—to obtain the present value for each year. The calculation of present values is simple using either a computer spreadsheet (Excel and others) or a programmed business calculator.

The sum of the annual cash flows, minus your initial $250,000 investment, equals a net present value of $15,300, as shown in the table. This is the value of the alternative above your costs, including the cost of capital. If you could sell the equipment at the end of five years—or get another year or two of positive cash flows from it—the alternative would be even more valuable.

To complete your analysis, you would determine the NPV of all other alternatives under consideration and then compare them. All other factors being equal, the alternative with the higher net present value is more financially attractive.

Some business people still use the *payback method*, which determines how long it will take to recoup your investment. Returning to the example in table 5-1, we see that at $70,000 in cash flows per year, the company's $250,000 investment in the new equipment will be recouped in roughly 3.5 years. That calculation is simple and straightforward, but it does not consider the company's cost of capital and the fact that one dollar of cash flow in the future is not as

TABLE 5-1

Net present value example (in thousands of dollars)

Year	0	1	2	3	4	5
Cash flows	−250	+70	+70	+70	+70	+70
PV at 10% discount rate	−250	+63.63	+57.82	+52.57	+47.81	+43.47
NPV = 15.3 (or $15,300)						

valuable as one dollar of cash flow today because of the time value of money. Because net present value considers those important factors, it is a superior tool of financial analysis.

Naturally, net present value is most useful when you can estimate future cash flows with some certainty. When those estimates are little more than guesswork, the power and utility of NPV for the decision maker crumble. Some analysts create best-case, worst-case, and most-likely-case scenarios to deal with the inherent difficulty of estimating future cash flows. These scenarios provide decision makers with a range of possible outcomes.

If you'd like to learn more about net present value analysis, consult any textbook on finance or turn to appendix B, which explains NPV in greater depth. That appendix also explains several other financial tools: breakeven analysis, sensitivity analysis, and internal rate of return (IRR), all of which have a place in decision making.

The Prioritization Matrix

Not all decisions are amenable to financial analysis. Often, values other than money are more significant. So how can you evaluate and compare alternatives? One approach is to use a *prioritization matrix,* which gives you a way to compare how well each alternative achieves your objectives. Like Franklin's system, a prioritization matrix uses weighted scores to rank each alternative; the alternative with the highest score is considered the best choice.

To create a prioritization matrix, begin by listing your objectives in making the decision. Then assign a value, or weight, to each (e.g., highest = 4). Next, rank each objective, along with its corresponding value, as a column header for your matrix, as shown in table 5-2. Assign a row in the matrix to each of your alternatives. Next, for each alternative, estimate how well it meets each of your objectives on a scale of 1 to 10 (10 = best possible); then multiply your estimate by the priority values. Add all the scores for each alternative to determine which has the highest number. Based on your priorities, this one is your best decision.

TABLE 5-2

The prioritization matrix

Alternative	Increase profits (4)	Maintain low customer costs (3)	Implement quickly (2)	Use few internal resources (1)	Total score
Alternative A	$9 \times 4 = 36$	$2 \times 3 = 6$	$7 \times 2 = 14$	$2 \times 1 = 2$	58
Alternative B	$2 \times 4 = 8$	$9 \times 3 = 27$	$8 \times 2 = 16$	$3 \times 1 = 3$	54

Source: Harvard ManageMentor® on Making Business Decisions, adapted with permission.

In this example, the highest-priority objective is "increase profits," so it is weighted as 4; "use few internal resources" has the lowest priority and is weighted as 1. Now notice that alternative A is given a high probability (9) of meeting the objective of increasing profits. If you multiply that estimate by the ranking you've assigned to this objective (4), the resulting score for alternative A in that square of the matrix is 36 ($9 \times 4 = 36$). As you can see, alternative A's total score is higher than alternative B's, making it a higher value to the company.

The Trade–off Table

Another method for comparing alternatives is the *trade-off table*. This table helps you identify the degree of variation between alternatives. Unlike the prioritization matrix, this one does not produce a numerical score. Instead, it visually juxtaposes key factors of the alternatives in a way that makes it easier to compare and mentally weight them, as Franklin recommended.

With this approach, you identify the important attributes of each alternative and compare them to each other. But instead of assigning priorities and estimates, as in the prioritization matrix, you use specific data. Table 5-3 is an example of a trade-off table, again using profits, customer costs, time to implement, and required internal resources as the key attributes of interest to decision makers.

TABLE 5-3

Trade-off table

Alternative	Profits	Customer costs	Time to implement	Internal resources
Alternative A	Profits increase by $100,000	Cost to customer increases by $1 per unit	6 months to implement	20 people required
Alternative B	Profits increase by $10,000	Cost to customer increases by $0	4 months to implement	15 people required

Source: Harvard ManageMentor® on Making Business Decisions, adapted with permission.

When you have laid out the alternatives with their associated information, consider how important these factors are to your company, and identify the trade-offs that you are willing to make. For example, in comparing alternatives A and B, would the $90,000 greater profits associated with alternative A be worth the cost and supervisory challenge of having five extra people on the payroll? Be sure to think about the trade-offs in light of the priority you assign to each objective.

Like the prioritization table, this trade-off table is an excellent device for getting people to talk about the various aspects of each choice. Obviously, different people will assign different weights as they prioritize various factors; they will argue about how long each alternative will take to implement and so forth. Talking about these differences is useful and informative, and it challenges people to produce empirical support for their views.

The trade-offs in table 5-3 suggest how this methodology can, and in many cases should, be supported with rigorous financial analysis. For example, the trade-off table estimates an increase in profit of $100,000 for alternative A. Net present value analysis would force the decision team to answer other relevant questions not addressed in the trade-off table: how long will it take to realize that increase? How long into the future can those profits be sustained? What magnitude of investment must the company make to obtain these results?

Decision Trees

A decision tree, another useful tool of analysis, is a visual representation of the alternative courses and their probable outcomes. Think of it as a road map of the various choices.

Figure 5-1 represents the decision tree for a company that is currently developing a new product. At this point, management must choose between two alternatives: A, abandon the project, and B, continue development.

Abandonment naturally leads to a dead end. Continuation, however, is bound to produce one of two outcomes: a successful product launch or a failed launch. Each of those outcomes has an associated probability (P). Probability represents a numerical estimate of the chance of an event occurring. In the figure, the probability of a successful product launch is estimated at 45 percent if the company continues the project. Generally, a decision team will ask each member (or other personnel who have experience with the situation) to provide individual estimates. These estimates are then averaged to arrive at the probability set in the decision tree.

In practice, the decision team would estimate not only the probability of outcomes but also their financial values.

FIGURE 5-1

Basic decision tree

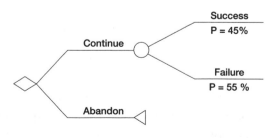

Source: George Wu, "Decision Analysis," Note 9-894-004 (Boston: Harvard Business School, revised December 4, 1997), 6. Adapted with permission.

Decision trees are helpful in graphically representing alternatives and their probable consequences, as estimated by the decision team and staff analysts. Shown on a whiteboard or screen, they become a centerpiece for discussion and debate. This approach works particularly well for investment decisions for which you can reasonably estimate the probability of various outcomes (such as success or failure) as well as the financial consequences.

Consider a typical example. You and your team must decide whether to continue manufacturing a component internally or to outsource the work to a supplier. A decision tree might present these alternatives as shown in figure 5-2. Based on this decision tree, the

FIGURE 5-2

Expanded decision tree

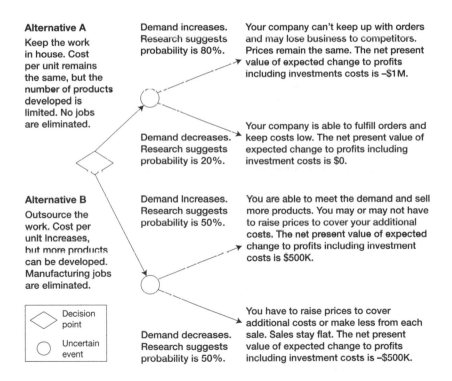

Alternative A

Keep the work in house. Cost per unit remains the same, but the number of products developed is limited. No jobs are eliminated.

Demand increases. Research suggests probability is 80%.

Your company can't keep up with orders and may lose business to competitors. Prices remain the same. The net present value of expected change to profits including investments costs is –$1M.

Demand decreases. Research suggests probability is 20%.

Your company is able to fulfill orders and keep costs low. The net present value of expected change to profits including investment costs is $0.

Alternative B

Outsource the work. Cost per unit increases, but more products can be developed. Manufacturing jobs are eliminated.

Demand Increases. Research suggests probability is 50%.

You are able to meet the demand and sell more products. You may or may not have to raise prices to cover your additional costs. The net present value of expected change to profits including investment costs is $500K.

Demand decreases. Research suggests probability is 50%.

You have to raise prices to cover additional costs or make less from each sale. Sales stay flat. The net present value of expected change to profits including investment costs is –$500K.

◇ Decision point

○ Uncertain event

Source: Harvard ManageMentor® on Making Business Decisions, adapted with permission.

best course of action would be to pursue alternative B. Of the two options, alternative B offers the highest risk-adjusted net present value. It is risk-adjusted by incorporation of the probability in the final financial result.

Decision trees typically are more robust than the two used in figure 5-2. More comprehensive decision trees evaluate more options and include multiple decision points. In general, the more alternatives you consider and the more complex the decision, the more likely you are to discover a solution that meets your needs.

A decision tree, however, does not automatically indicate the best course of action; you still need to assess the information in the tree. Moreover, the probabilities and financial estimates indicated in the decision tree must be realistic and, where possible, based on available data.

Computers to the Rescue

A good decision, according to Alan Rowe, depends on managers' ability to make sense of the information at their disposal, something that is extremely difficult when information is voluminous and comes from many unrelated sources. In these cases, decision makers may need the help of computers to sort through data, array them in useful ways, and do some number crunching. "Managers rely on their perceptions and cognitive abilities when using information," write Rowe and coauthor Sue Anne Davis. "Where perception or cognition limits their effectiveness, an Intelligent Information System can supplement their abilities."[3] In a complex world, decision makers can be confused, befuddled, or even paralyzed by mountains of unstructured information. That's where computers and decision software come to the rescue.

Since they first came into use, say Rowe and Davis, computers have progressed from simply storing and regurgitating information to more sophisticated work, such as simulating and predicting outcomes. Indeed, technology has come to the aid of managers in the form of decision-making software tools. Some of the currently available tools focus on specific analytical techniques, such as decision trees. Others allow users to model alternative scenarios and run simulations; some of these are tailored to the needs of specific industries, such as insurance underwriting, commercial lending, and energy industry portfolio management. The simplest of these software tools are affordable and can be purchased off-the-shelf.

David Matheson, CEO of SmartOrg, a decision-support software producer in Menlo Park, California, categorizes these tools into four groups. The first and simplest is what he calls product-choice software. Chances are that you've encountered this type of decision tool if you've gone shopping online for a new camera or similar product. The tool asks you a set of questions about your buying preferences: your photo-taking skills, the intended applications, option and price preferences, the number of megapixels required (for digital imaging), and so forth. After a second or two of crunching, the program produces a short list of available cameras that should meet your needs.

Insurance companies and lending institutions have developed similar but more complex "expert systems" to aid their decision making. One of the first of these was used to make insurance underwriting specialists more efficient and effective in their decisions. That software system checked the applications submitted by potential policyholders against a set of standards that supported either issuing or not issuing the policy. For example, if an applicant indicated a history of early heart disease in his family or if he had more than two moving violations on his driving record, the system would automatically register a certain number of negative points against the applicant. In handling these simpler issues quickly and accurately, the software allowed the underwriters to focus their time and attention on more difficult and ambiguous issues and hopefully helped them make better decisions. Many loan applications are now handled with similar decision-assisting software.

Matheson points to group productivity software as the second major class of decision-support software. This software helps members of decision groups communicate their preferences to others and identify issues on which they agree and disagree. For example, a team of advertising managers and creative personnel can use this software in connection with voting pad devices to indicate the level of individual support for the many elements that go into a multimedia ad program. Group members can quickly identify the issues on which they agree and disagree—as well as the magnitude of their feelings. They can then concentrate their thinking and discussion on areas of divergence.

Decision analysis software is the third class described by Matheson. This type of software might be used, for example, to simplify the construction of decision trees and risk measurement. It might also assist a decision team in modeling and quantifying the dozens of important factors that influence an outcome. Alternatively, it might be used with an electronic spreadsheet to model the income statement of a planned project, making it possible to observe the bottom-line consequences of various revenue or cost scenarios: the classic "what if" exercise.

The most complex form of decision software is what Matheson calls enterprise decision tools. These dynamic systems incorporate probabilities and forecast cash flows and many other factors. Smart-Org's "value-based management systems," for instance, were developed to help R&D organizations identify and manage the risks and value drivers within individual projects and within entire R&D portfolios. One feature, for example, graphically indicates the impact of each uncertainty (e.g., variable costs, pricing) on a project's net present value. This makes it easy to see which uncertainties are potentially the most dangerous and which are trivial. Another feature ranks all projects in the R&D portfolio in terms of investment return. Such features help managers make decisions about which projects to fund and which to kill. And for a large, R&D-intensive company, those decisions are worth many millions.

Chances are that you are already using some type of decision software, even if it's only an Excel spreadsheet used to create a pro forma income statement for the coming year. That's a good start, but more elaborate tools are available (see "Want to Learn More About

> ## *Want to Learn More About Decision Software?*
>
> Many decision software tools are now available. Many of them use spreadsheets, decision trees, influence diagrams, and other advanced techniques. To review what's available, check out the following Web site, which is provided by the Decision Analysis Society and hosted by the Fuqua School of Business at Duke University: http://faculty.fuqua.duke.edu/daweb/dasw.htm.

Decision Software?"). You should become familiar with those that can help your business.

The Problem of Uncertainty

As you evaluate alternatives, you'll notice that some are more uncertain than others. For example, alternative C may have a much higher potential return for the company than alternative D. But C's return many depend on assumptions and cost estimates that may or may not hold, whereas D is almost a sure thing.

In business, uncertainty of outcome is synonymous with risk, and you must factor it into your evaluation. We touched on it briefly in our discussion of probability. There is much, much more to uncertainty that you need to consider—so much that we've made uncertainty the subject of its own chapter (chapter 7).

The task of evaluating alternatives is more effective when you have a systematic approach and rigorous tools at hand (see "Tips for Evaluating Alternatives"). If you are able to adapt the tools described here to your business, you'll be in a better position to make a good decision. However, always keep in mind the objective you have set out to achieve, and focus on it as you evaluate each alternative.

Tips for Evaluating Alternatives

- Ask the most respected and objective members of the decision team to act as devil's advocates. Their job is to make a case against the group's preferred proposals. Ask them to explain in detail why the preferred option should *not* be adopted.

- Acknowledge and discuss minority points of view whenever possible. Try to include more than one person in your group who is likely to express a minority opinion. A single person who disagrees with the majority is far less effective than multiple dissenting voices. A lone dissenter may be reluctant to speak up.

Summing Up

- The goal of evaluating alternatives should be to estimate how well each choice meets the objective you established at the outset.

- When strategic and capital budgeting decisions are at stake, you should scrutinize alternatives in terms of financial measures of value. Net present value (NPV) is the key measure.

- Net present value is the sum of the present value of one or more future cash flows minus any initial investment costs.

- A prioritization matrix provides a way to compare how well each alternative achieves your objectives. You create this graphic by first listing each objective and assigning it a weight, or value. Then you estimate how well each alternative meets those objectives using a scale from 1 to 10. A process of multiplication and summing determines the total score of each alternative, and the one with the highest score is the most successful in meeting the company's priorities.

- A trade-off table is a method for comparing the important attributes of your alternatives.

- A decision tree is a visual representation of the alternative courses of action and their probable outcomes. You can quantify the value of those outcomes by assigning probabilities to the estimated financial results.

- Specialized software has been developed to help decision makers collect and array data and crunch numbers.

6

Make the Decision

Getting to Agreement

Key Topics Covered in This Chapter

- *How to use three techniques for moving a group toward a decision*

- *The dangers of making a decision too early—or too late*

- *The first step of decision implementation*

C HAPTER 5 OUTLINES several techniques for evaluating alternatives. These techniques can help you compare the pros and cons of each choice. However, they do not dictate which decision should be made because people on the decision team may have different views of the evaluations. In addition, subjective and qualitative concerns may not be fully addressed in the evaluation process. Consequently, useful as well as subversive considerations are likely to creep in.

The decision team must take its evaluations and conflicting opinions and move on to the next step: making a decision. This chapter describes three techniques that you can use in moving toward closure on a difficult decision. It also moves beyond the decision to the steps that management must take in communicating the decision and involving those who will be responsible for implementing it.

Three Decision–Making Techniques

Based on the process, your decision team should be in agreement on its objective and on the importance of the issue at hand. There should be no hidden or self-serving agendas; all relevant facts, uncertainties, and issues should be on the table. Given this situation, team members can objectively examine the alternatives and their respective evaluations. Like wise judges, they will sift through the evidence, weigh the pros and cons, and move on toward a decision.

But it isn't always that easy. Some people may be committed to one option. Others may have trouble weighing the merits and short-comings of the alternatives. Still others many disagree with basic assumptions. In addition, unresolved uncertainties are bound to trouble some decision makers. Fortunately, there are techniques that can help the decision team get through these difficulties: catchball, point-counterpoint, and intellectual watchdog. We explain them in this section.

Catchball

Catchball is one of the many management methods developed in Japan over the past several decades. It is a cross-functional method for accomplishing two things: improving ideas and encouraging buy-in among participants.[1]

Here's how it works. An initial idea is "tossed" to a collaborator for consideration, as in figure 6-1. The idea might be a new market-ing strategy, a new product, or a way to improve a work process. Whoever "catches" the idea assumes responsibility for understand-ing it and improving it in some way.

For example, suppose the idea in question is an initial market testing plan for a new line of PC storage devices. The person who "catches" the plan will take the time to understand and refine it.

FIGURE 6-1

Catchball

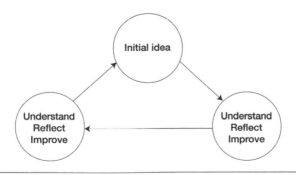

That person then tosses the improved idea back to the group, where it is caught by another person and, hopefully, improved still further. And around it goes, in a cycle of gradual improvement until people are satisfied that meaningful improvement can no longer be made. As people participate, they develop a sense of shared responsibility and commitment to the idea that gradually emerges—and these feelings of ownership help when the time comes to implement the decision.

You can use this same approach as a means of closing in on a difficult decision. Consider, for example, how a decision-making team might use catchball to select the best alternative for acquiring and maintaining the company's fleet of automobiles. The company needs to decide whether to renew its current leasing arrangement, select another lease company, or purchase its vehicles outright.

> *After considering all factors, Helen favored a renewal of the current lease with LeaseCo (all names in this example are fictitious). "There's a lot of merit in the idea of switching from LeaseCo to Consolidated Motors," she told the others. "Consolidated's terms are measurably better, but we can't be sure of the quality of their maintenance, despite their contract terms and verbal assurances. I keep thinking of the old expression, 'Better the devil you know than the devil you don't know.' That's why I favor renewing our current lease."*
>
> *Karl took up the problem. "Yes, there's an uncertainty issue here," he agreed. "We'll never really know how good a vendor Consolidated is until we've committed to them. Still, I'd hate to let $45,000 in annual savings slip through our fingers." Karl asked the team if they would put off the decision for one week while he tried to clear up the uncertainty about Consolidated's performance. That afternoon, he asked one of his subordinates to investigate. "Get the names of ten or twelve companies that currently operate auto fleets leased from Consolidated," he said. "Then get on the phone and contact the person most involved in the deal." Karl then handed his subordinate a list of five questions regarding customer satisfaction and Consolidated's performance. "I need the information by early next week."*
>
> *At the decision team's next meeting, Karl reported his findings. Everyone was pleased with how the additional information closed an uncertainty gap, making it easier to reach a decision.*

One of the virtues of catchball is that each "catcher" assumes responsibility for taking an action that will improve the likelihood of a good decision. In the example, Karl did this by acquiring previously unavailable information. That information cleared up an important source of uncertainty for the decision team.

Point–Counterpoint

Point-counterpoint involves the same principle of iterative improvement but involves two teams. Here's how you can use it.

1. Divide your decision team into two groups of equal size: group A and group B. Be sure to include supporters of opposing ideas in each group.

2. Group A proposes a decision. Its written proposal should include recommendations, key assumptions, and supporting data.

3. Group A presents its proposal to group B in a meeting.

4. Group B identifies one or more alternative courses of action, documenting its key assumptions and gathering supporting data.

5. Group B presents its ideas to group A in a second meeting.

6. In a third meeting, both groups debate the two proposals and identify a common set of assumptions. Manage the meeting so that the two groups continue to debate a variety of options based on common assumptions. The ultimate goal is to get the whole group to agree on a recommendation.

This is an excellent way to ensure that all points of view and all personal insights are included. Consider this example:

The finance department of Gizmo Products, Inc., has been engaged in a heated debate over which accounting firm to use to audit its books this year (again, all the names in this example are fictitious). One group favors one of the big-name national firms, whereas the other favors a smaller but well-respected local firm. They are deadlocked and unable to reach a decision that most people would support. The CFO does not want to impose his view on his subordinates. "We need a decision that most people can live with," he says. "That's how we operate around here."

Using the point-counterpoint technique, the decision-making team breaks into two groups, each containing supporters of the opposing views. One group develops a decision proposal, which the other considers and then returns to the first group for evaluation and improvement. Eventually, they reach a conclusion that reflects the insights of all participants and that all can accept.

At first glance, one might think that the two groups would be as deadlocked as the department as a whole. After all, each group contains members who support opposing viewpoints. But small groups have a strange chemistry that often leads to consensus, something that's harder to generate in larger groups.

Intellectual Watchdog

Similar to the point-counterpoint technique, the *intellectual watchdog* technique begins by dividing the decision team into two groups. But instead of asking each to develop a counterproposal, you ask one group to critique and ask for improvement in the other's approach.

Here are the steps for using this technique:

1. Divide your team into two groups of equal size: group A and group B.

2. Group A develops a written proposal for its decision. The proposal should include recommendations, key assumptions, and supporting data.

3. Group A presents its proposal to group B in a meeting.

4. Group B develops a detailed written critique of group A's assumptions and recommendations.

5. Group B presents its critique to group A in a second meeting.

6. Group A revises its proposal based on group B's feedback.

7. Group A presents its revised proposal in a third meeting.

8. Subsequent meetings are held in which the two groups continue to critique and revise the proposal until they agree on a recommendation.

Here's an example of the intellectual watchdog technique at work:

A manufacturer of office furniture needs to improve the quality of its products, and two groups are assigned to work on the problem using the point-counterpoint approach. The first group assumes that the company's quality problems stem from outdated manufacturing equipment; its recommendation is an investment in computer-controlled equipment. It develops a written document that explains why equipment is the problem and includes a cost-benefit analysis of the $2 million investment it believes necessary to cure the problem.

Members of the second group question the assumptions of their colleagues, as well as the $2 million estimate. They present their critique in written form to the first group. The first group then revises its proposal, and the two groups work together in the revision-critique-revision cycle until they arrive at a solution that both groups feel will improve their products' quality.

Other Ways to Resolve Disagreements and Reach Closure

Despite their usefulness, neither catchball, point-counterpoint, nor the intellectual watchdog technique can guarantee that your decision team will agree on a decision. However, if the leader maintains the focus of both groups on their common goal and insists on an objective treatment of the proposals that emerge, a decision should be within reach. Failing this, one of the following steps might help:

- Revisit and reexamine assumptions.

- Go back to your original objective and ensure that it remains relevant, given the decision you plan to make.

- Set a deadline. For example, "By next Tuesday we will make our decision, no matter how much uncertainty remains." Unfortunately, some people will talk and debate endlessly without a specific deadline.

- Agree in advance that if disagreements are unresolved, the choice will be made by the boss or by a majority vote. People who have been dragging their heels may change their behavior if they understand that the decision may be taken out of their hands.

Ending Deliberations

Knowing when to end deliberations is often difficult. If you make a decision too early, you might not explore every promising possibility. If you sense that your group is rushing to make a decision, it's best to slow things down. Consider adjourning your meeting before making a final choice and then reconvene at a later time. Ask each participant to try to find a flaw with the decision the group was about to make and present it at the next meeting.

The flip side of deciding too early is deciding too late, which is equally problematic. In making a decision too late you will waste valuable time and possibly miss the opportunity you're trying to seize. Teams that insist on hearing every viewpoint, resolving every question, and chasing down every last piece of information before reaching a conclusion often fall into a tiresome, endless loop. If you find that your group is going around in circles, it is your job as a manager to bring the discussion to closure. You may need to force the issue by establishing a deadline for a decision, using the best information available at that time.

After the Decision

A decision—especially an important one—is a milestone and not the end of the road. After a decision is made, you need to turn it into action. Implementation is beyond the scope of this *Essentials* book, but the first step of implementation, communication, is not. The way you communicate the decision will to some degree determine your success. As you communicate, show consideration for the views of others, explain the thinking behind your decision, state your post-decision expectations, and notify all the right people of the decision you've made.

Show Consideration

If participants are genuinely encouraged to question and debate each other's ideas, they are more likely to believe that their own viewpoints will be given serious consideration, especially if the leader has demonstrated attentiveness through her actions—for example, by taking notes and paraphrasing what was said to show she was actively listening. Even if the participants' viewpoints did not prevail, knowing that they were taken seriously will lend credibility to the process and acceptance of the final decision.

Some managers, unfortunately, try to shortcut their obligation to consider the views of others by falsely giving the impression that others' views are factored into decision. Consider this example:

> *Lester convened a staff meeting every Monday morning to identify issues of concern and to make decisions about the work ahead. He presided, and his four direct reports participated. It didn't take long, however, for his reports to notice that Lester's ideas always prevailed. He would solicit their ideas, and they'd talk them through. But in the end, Lester made all the decisions and always got his way. "What's the point of this charade?" complained one of Lester's subordinates to another. "Why doesn't he drop the pretense and simply tell us what he's decided?"*

Don't be like Lester. If you invite others to participate in decisions, that invitation must be genuine. If you run a charade, you'll lose respect and cooperation, and the best of your people will eventually leave for greener pastures.

Explain the Decision

Always explain the thinking behind a final decision. It's important to be clear about why that alternative was chosen, as opposed to others.

Explaining builds trust in the leadership's intentions and confidence that the choice was made for the benefit of the company as a whole. If you don't do this, people will ask themselves, "Why didn't she even consider my point of view?"

Manage Post–Decision Expectations

After the decision has been made, everyone affected by the decision must understand the decision and its consequences. New responsibilities need to be spelled out, as do performance expectations and penalties for failure. When people clearly understand expectations, they can focus on what needs to be done.

Notify the Right People

Notify everyone who is responsible for implementing the decision as well as anyone affected by it. Your list might also include the key stakeholders: members of your unit who were not part of the decision-making group, as well as senior management, department supervisors, external constituents, and even customers if they will see a change in the way you do business with them.

Your message to these individuals should include the following:

- **A statement of the issue that was addressed.** "Our bonus policy hasn't effectively differentiated between high and low performers. The bonus checks of our top quartile performers are not much higher than those of the bottom quartile."

- **A description of the objectives or decision–making criteria.** "We set out with a clear objective: to restructure the bonus system to reward people for their real contributions."

- **The names and roles of the people involved in making the decision and why they were included.** "Our decision team included people with special insights into the issue: Sharon Henderson, director of benefits and compensation, Stan Halloway, our COO . . . "

- **The alternatives considered (and possibly a summary of the analysis in table form).** "After a period of benchmarking best-practice companies, we zeroed in on the three options shown in this overhead . . . "

- **An explanation of the final decision and what it means for the key stakeholders.** "In the end, we found option B to be the best choice, given our objective of scaling bonuses to measurable contributions. Sharon will explain how it's structured and what it means for you."

- **The implementation plan and time frame.** "Everyone who is eligible for the bonus plan will receive a brochure explaining how it works and how it's tied to our system of performance reviews. It will go into effect at the beginning of the next quarter."

- **Recognition of those who participated.** "This new plan reflects the ideas and the hard work of many people. Every Gizmo Products employee owes them thanks for their contributions."

- **Solicitation of feedback.** "One of the things we learned is that no bonus system is perfect. This one may not be perfect either. And we'll know more about its imperfections as we implement it over time. So we encourage feedback from you, the people affected by this decision. As you see ways to better achieve our objective of rewarding performance, tell me, tell Sharon, tell your boss. Your ideas matter in this company."

Be sure to take the time to create a clear, concise message. An incomplete or poorly articulated message about the decision can lead to confusion, disappointment, and unwillingness to support implementation.

After a final choice has been made, some members of the decision team will have to give up their preferred solutions. If they perceive the decision-making process as fair, however, this shouldn't be a problem. There's plenty of evidence that perceived fairness goes a long way in defusing opposition, creating legitimacy, and paving the way for support. For more on this issue, see "Tips for Promoting a Fair Process."

Tips for Promoting a Fair Process

Here are things you can do to ensure that your process is both fair and perceived as fair.

- Listen attentively to people who don't share your ideas, and be patient when others explain theirs. Try not to interrupt. Doing otherwise gives the appearance that you are railroading the decision.

- Make eye contact with other decision team members, and nod your head to indicate that you hear what they are saying.

- Either take notes yourself or appoint a note taker to show that everyone's ideas are valued and respected—and are part of the record.

- Make it clear from the outset that even though not all of the group's suggestions will be adopted, all of them will be considered fairly.

- Ask targeted questions to promote understanding, foster debate, and prompt new ideas.

- When you ask a question or move the conversation in a different direction, repeat the main idea of an individual's comments. For example, "You make a good point. Vendor A does have excellent references. Do others share these views of vendor A? Has anyone identified any flaws in vendor A's proposal?"

- If you are responsible for making the final decision (instead of having a consensus or majority vote), let the group members know how their ideas affected the final decision, or explain why you chose to differ with them.

We've now covered the entire five-step decision-making process: establishing the context, framing the problem, generating alternatives, evaluating alternatives, and making the decision. This process can be applied to decisions of all types and sizes. In the remaining chapters we circle back and examine in detail some of the knottier issues faced by decision makers, beginning with uncertainty.

Summing Up

- Catchball is a method for improving ideas and creating buy-in among participants. Whoever "catches" the idea assumes responsibility for understanding it and improving it in some way before passing it on to someone else in the decision group.

- Point-counterpoint involves the same principle of iterative improvement as catchball but is different in that it involves two teams. Each is asked to develop a counterproposal.

- The intellectual watchdog technique, like point-counterpoint, divides the decision team into two groups. But instead of asking each to develop a set of counterproposals, one group is asked to critique and identify possible improvements in the other's approach.

- Take care to avoid ending deliberations too early or too late. Ending too early may leave promising opportunities unexplored. Ending too late wastes time and may cause your decision team to miss a fleeting opportunity.

- After you've made a decision, you must begin implementing it. The first step of implementation is communication. As you communicate, show consideration for the views of others, explain the thinking behind your decision, state your post-decision expectations, and notify all the right people of the decision you've made.

- Implementation will be more successful if the people affected by it view the decision process as fair.

7

The Uncertainty Problem

How to Deal with Unknowns

Key Topics Covered in This Chapter

- *A three-step process for dealing with decision uncertainty*

- *Business tactics for dealing with uncertainty*

- *How and when to follow your intuition*

I F YOU ARE LIKE most people, uncertainty—that is, risk—is a major impediment to making good decisions—or to making decisions at all. Every decision involves a trip through foggy patches of uncertainty because decisions are about the future, an unwritten story for which there are no facts.

Most of us rely on what we know about the past to provide insights into the future. What we know of the past and the present can help us understand where we are, where we have been, and what the general trajectory of our journey looks like. But the past and present provide nothing more than hints about the future. As Coleridge put it, "History is a lantern at the stern of a ship, revealing only where it has been," casting only a dim light on the course ahead.

Consider these typical examples of decision uncertainties:

Yes, we can raise our prices, but how will our customers respond?

Should I order one thousand units or five thousand? I'll get a volume discount on the larger order, and that will save me money on every unit. That's certain. But I'm not sure I can sell five thousand without cutting the price.

We like this strategic plan. It seems sound, and it will differentiate us in a way that customers will appreciate. But our competitors aren't stupid; they won't sit on their hands and let us run all over them. Can anyone tell me what our competitors are likely to do to counter our new strategy? Perhaps they are already making moves we don't know about.

Given the current exchange rate, I should buy a $100,000 ten-year U.S. Treasury note. My euros can buy more in the United States for less than they could last year. But if the U.S. dollar continues to weaken against the euro, the buying power of my interest income here in Europe will drop with it. Can anyone tell me what the exchange rate will be next year, or five years from now, or ten?

This chapter addresses the knotty problem of uncertainty and offers a three-step approach for dealing with it:

Step 1: Identify the areas of uncertainty.

Step 2: Determine which uncertainties could have the greatest impact on the outcome of your decision.

Step 3: Reduce key uncertainties to the extent that you have the time and resources to do so.

These steps cannot solve the problem of uncertainty, but they can help reduce its extent and improve the odds of making a good decision.

Finally, there's the issue of intuition. What does your "gut" tell you when uncertainty stares you in the face—or when supposedly reliable facts are presented to you? Do you find yourself saying, "The numbers make sense, but I have a bad feeling about this"? We'll explore this difficult area and end with an example of how you can get the empirical and intuitive parts of your brain working together.

But first, we will consider the three steps for dealing with uncertainty.

Step 1: Identify Areas of Uncertainty

It's difficult to imagine an important decision for which you have all the information you need to evaluate alternatives and move toward an optimum choice. Can you think of even one? Certainty in one area or another is always missing. Here are some examples:

• Future customer preferences

• The impact of new technologies

- Counter moves by competitors

- Technical success in your R&D lab

- The availability of capital when you need it

Where are the areas of uncertainty in the decisions you are trying to make?

Ideally, the time to identify uncertainties is in the evaluation phase of the decision-making process. Dealing with the unknowns too early will discourage people from developing a list of creative alternatives. A typical response might be, "Forget that one—there would be too many unknowns to get a go-ahead from senior management."

The evaluation phase requires a systematic identification and listing of the uncertainties associated with each alternative. A matrix like the one shown in table 7-1, which describes alternative versions of a new consumer product, can help you to be systematic in capturing all the uncertainties in a single place.

The uncertainties listed in the matrix should be based on the input of experienced people: sales representatives, manufacturing managers, and whoever else has insights into the issue. Try your hand at creating a similar matrix for the alternatives you are currently evaluating. Think, too, about the individuals who could help you enumerate all the uncertainties.

Ask for Ranges

Notice in table 7-1 that each category of uncertainty is expressed as a range. Point estimates are not given, and wisely so, because point estimates are almost always wrong. Worse, point estimates give the impression of certainty when there is none. What the decision maker needs is a range of possible outcomes for each uncertainty, as determined by experienced and knowledgeable informants.

> *"Can someone give me an estimate of the manufacturing cost of alternative A?" asked the CEO.*
>
> *"We cannot say for certain," responded Margaret, the manufacturing delegate to the decision team. "We won't have all the specifications until we get through the prototype phase."*

TABLE 7-1

Listing of uncertainties

Risk	Alternative A	Alternative B	Alternative C
First-year unit sales	35,000–75,000	40,000–70,000	70,000–80,000
Net unit sales revenue	$15–$20	$15–$20	$12–$15
Manufacturing cost per unit	$6–$6.50	$5–$8	$5–$6
Time to commercialize	8–12 months	10–12 months	4–6 months

"I wouldn't expect an exact number at this stage," the CEO continued. "But based on the information available to you at this time, what costs are we likely to encounter?"

"We've estimated six to seven euros per unit."

To appreciate the importance of range estimates—as opposed to point estimates—consider the statistical analogy: variation from the mean (average). An average is a point of data, but it contains limited information about the data set from which it is derived. For example, consider the people who ride the bus that leaves your corner at 8 a.m. each morning. If you wanted to know something about those people, you could weigh each passenger, add up their individual weights, and then divide by the number of passengers. In effect, you'd have calculated the average weight of those bus riders—a single number. Let's say that the average was 160 pounds. That single number, however, wouldn't tell you everything you need to know about the weight of the people who ride the bus. All of them might weigh very close to 160 pounds—say, between 150 and 170 pounds. Or there might be a great many who weigh less than 110, with a few tipping the scales at 250 pounds or more. In either case the average would be 160. If you're a decision maker, that number may or may not tell you what you need to know about the bus passengers. In fact, it's likely that *not one* of them actually weighs 160 pounds. Knowing the range of individual weights, in contrast, would give you a better sense of the weight of the people riding the bus.

When your decision team evaluates its alternatives, do you seek point estimates, or do you look for ranges of possible outcomes? Simply acknowledging that point estimates are almost always wrong is one of the best defenses against making a bad decision.

Assign Probabilities

In some cases, a range will not do. Instead, one or another thing will or will not happen. For example, the successful development of a new product may hinge on the success of a laboratory prototype—which will either work or fail.

We encountered probabilities earlier in our discussion of decision trees. Let's revisit decision trees and develop that concept a bit further. Consider the decision tree in figure 7-1. Here, managers are faced with a string of possibilities, each with its own estimated probability. In the first decision, the managers must choose either to proceed with the development of a new product or to abandon the project. What could happen if the choice were made to proceed? The answer is that the product prototype will either work or fail. In the collective judgment of technical people, the probability that it will work is 60 percent. After that bridge is crossed, the company would continue development, with the goal being a commercially

FIGURE 7-1

Probabilities are cumulative

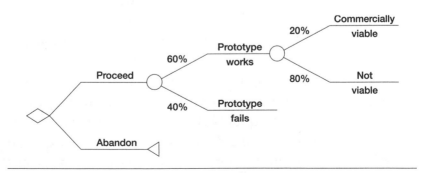

viable product it can launch into the marketplace. They estimate only a 20 percent chance of this happening.

Now if you multiply the probabilities of these two outcomes, you will have the overall probability of actually putting a product on the market:

60% P of prototype success × 20% P of developing
a launchworthy project = 12%

Step 2: Determine Which Uncertainties Could Have the Greatest Impact

It goes without saying that some uncertainties will have a greater impact on the value of a decision than will others. One uncertainty might merely reduce your profit margin if the future doesn't unfold as anticipated. Another uncertainty, however, might hand you a multimillion-dollar loss. The job of the decision maker is to sort out the likelihood of each decision as well as its potential impact.

Referring to table 7-1, the greatest uncertainty is the estimated number of units to be sold in the first year. Alternative A is particularly risky on this score. The likely cost of manufacturing alternative A, on the other hand, has a narrow range. In this example, whether the high or low estimate occurred—$6.00 versus $6.50—wouldn't have much impact on operating profits.

This result might seem obvious, but we're using an obvious example to make the point. In real life, the potential impact of some uncertainties on the outcome of a decision are not readily apparent. In those cases, decision makers could make the mistake of fretting over uncertainties that matter very little while ignoring the ones that could cause serious harm.

One way to use the data in this example is to multiply the low unit-sales estimate for each alternative by its respective low net-revenue estimate. Then do the same with the high unit-sales and high unit-revenue figures. What you get is a range of net revenues for each alternative from best case to worst case, as shown in table 7-2.

TABLE 7-2

Range of impacts on revenue

Range	Alternative A	Alternative B	Alternative C
Low	35,000 units × $15 per unit = $0.525 million	40,000 units × $15 per unit = $0.6 million	70,000 units × $12 per unit = $0.84 million
High	75,000 units × $20 per unit = $1.5 million	70,000 units × $20 per unit = $1.4 million	80,000 units × $15 per unit = $1.2 million
Revenue estimates (millions)	$0.525–$1.5	$0.6–$1.4	$0.84–$1.2

This information gives a clearer picture of the potential impact of each of the alternatives being considered; alternative A contains the broadest range of possible outcomes, and alternative C contains the narrowest range.

You could sharpen this picture still further by calculating the impact of manufacturing costs on these same ranges. Doing so will bring your analysis closer to the bottom-line effect of each alternative.

Step 3: Attempt to Reduce Key Uncertainties

Once you know the most important uncertainties—the ones that could really hurt you—you will be in a better position to allocate scarce time and financial resources to reducing those areas of uncertainty. Here are some of the techniques that companies use to reduce uncertainties:

• Customer research

• Test marketing of new products in selected cities

• Focus group interviews

• Direct observation of how customers use products

• Computer simulations

McDonald's, for example, owns and operates a number of restaurants (most are owned by franchisees) that it uses to test customer acceptance of new menu items before it makes the decision to introduce them broadly. This testing takes time and resources, but it reduces the risk in the company's decisions. Other companies use sophisticated methods such as conjoint analysis (mapping how consumers see the relative value of product features) to test customer willingness to trade off one value for another. These and other methods shed light on murky areas where decision makers must operate.

Many decision uncertainties involve future customer preferences (what will they want?) and levels of future customer demand (how many will they want?). The first is critical for decisions about developing products and services; the second affects recurring decisions about production and inventory. Although most people try to clarify these uncertainties through market research, some companies have found tactical methods for reducing them. Here we look at four of these methods: narrowing time gaps, building to order, risk-limiting tactics, and staged decisions.

Narrow Time Gaps

In the early 1990s, researchers at Harvard Business School discovered an important difference between Japanese and American automakers: the Japanese were designing and launching new car models in roughly two years, whereas their U.S. competitors took almost four years to do the same thing. Being faster to market gave the Japanese certain advantages. The most obvious was that they began receiving revenues from their new model investments much sooner. The Americans faced four years of expenses before they earned a dollar from their work. But there was another, less obvious benefit from cutting time to market: less uncertainty.

Uncertainty for the Japanese was lower because they had to anticipate customer needs and preferences only two years down the road—a reasonable planning horizon—instead of four years. Also, the technologies they designed into their vehicles were likely to be fresh and exciting two years in the future, when newly designed models hit dealer showrooms. Ford, General Motors, and Chrysler (now DaimlerChrysler), in contrast, had to anticipate what customers would want four years in the future—a vastly more speculative task. And the technologies they adopted for their vehicles risked being outdated by the time their new models reached the showroom. These problems raised the risks of producing new models.

How long does it take your company to design and launch a new product? A year? Three years? Five? Whatever it is, you can reduce some of the uncertainty by reducing the time gap between your decision and its implementation. Just as our vision becomes less clear as we turn our eyes from our immediate vicinity to the distant horizon, planning horizons become increasingly uncertain as they extend into the future.

Perhaps no company has learned and acted on this lesson more capably than Zara, a successful Spanish designer and manufacturer of fashionable clothing. Clothing fashions are notoriously short-lived—a moving target—with the result that manufacturers that are late getting their clothing to market miss sales and are stuck with inventory. Zara has countered both problems by developing a customer intelligence system for finding out what's hot, and a manufacturing process capable of getting new designs to market in less than two weeks, before hot fashions turn cold. This system cuts some of the risk of product decisions. As David Bovet and Joseph Martha have described in their supply-chain book *Value Nets*, "Zara's ability to bring new designs to stores in less than two weeks allows it to carry less inventory and minimize accumulations of stock due to suppy-demand mismatch."[1]

Build to Order

Fashion isn't the only field in which demand uncertainties plague managers. Industries from homebuilding to computers face the same problem. Another way to reduce uncertainty is to adopt a build-to-order strategy. Following this strategy, decision makers don't have to gamble with how many products to build or how to configure them. Those decisions are made by customers in advance of production.

Not every company can follow a build-to-order strategy because its customers will not wait a week, a month, or longer to take delivery; they want it quickly. But of those who can build to order, few have succeeded as famously as Dell, the world's largest maker of personal computers. Dell managers are not burdened by decisions about how many machines to build and which features to include. Customers make those decisions for them every day. Dell's supply chain swings into action only when an order is taken and the exact specifications are known. That supply chain is so efficient that Dell can deliver a custom-built machine to a customer's doorstep in ten days or less. Rivals who build to stock, in contrast, often make too many of what customers don't really want and end up with lots of unwanted inventory. And in the PC industry, the value of inventory deteriorates at an amazing rate of 2 percent per day. These manufacturers also risk making too few of the machines that customers want in a given month, and that results in missed sales.

Is a build-to-order strategy possible for your company? If it is, you can eliminate substantial uncertainty from your production decisions. If your company cannot build to order, there is a compromise solution: build items to stock with all but the finishing details added as orders come in. Benetton popularized this strategy in the clothing industry. Benetton makes sweaters, for example, from undyed material. Once the season's popular colors are known, it quickly dyes its semifinished stock and ships it out, thereby cutting the time between the receipt of market information and the shipment of its products and reducing the risk of producing items in unpopular colors.

Adopt Risk–Limiting Production Tactics

Even when decision makers lack sound data, it's often possible to limit risk. A developer and manufacturer of music compact discs, for example, will have only a vague idea of how many copies will be ordered during the first year. Every CD experiences a different level of customer demand. Prerelease orders from music stores is one indicator of demand, but it's unreliable at best. Nevertheless, someone must decide on an initial production run.

One practical way to limit risk is to manufacture enough copies to satisfy prerelease sales *plus* six or eight thousand extras, and then be prepared to restock quickly if sales take off. This strategy will reduce two risks: the risk of producing too many CDs (and ending up with worthless inventory) and the risk of producing too few (and missing sales because of an out-of-stock condition).

Most other decisions provide similar opportunities to reduce risk. Consider one of the most problem-plagued areas of decision making: hiring. A bad hiring decision can cost a company royally— $140 million, in the case of Disney's ill-fated hiring of Michael Ovitz. Even a poorly performing middle-level manager can cost an employer $1 million or more in severance, recruiting, and business mistakes. Because the true value of a new employee can be known only after that person is on the payroll and in the job, many employers have an official probationary period of two to four months during which the new person's performance is regularly monitored. He can be terminated during that period without the reviews, remediation efforts, and separation costs normally accorded to long-term employees.

Other firms have taken an additional risk-reducing step: they hire people as independent contractors to handle temporary jobs. If the temp worker demonstrates good performance, the company hires her to a full-time position.

Make Staged Decisions

Venture capitalists (VCs) take substantial risks when they fund young, entrepreneurial businesses. Few business investments, in fact, are made with so little in the way of rock-solid information. In many cases the only facts VCs have to work with are a business plan and the reputation of the start-up company's founder and management team.

The level of uncertainty in these situations is very high. Yet budding enterprises need several million dollars in cash to get off the ground. How do VCs contain their risks? In most cases they make their cash contributions through a set of staged decisions.

Each decision in the sequence is treated as an experiment, a practice that produces learning that feeds into the next decision (see figure 7-2). For example, if the new business needs $1 million in venture capital, a VC may provide an initial investment of $200,000 and then set up a set of milestones that must be reached within a certain period. When that time comes, the business's progress and current circumstances are reevaluated, and another go–no go decision will be made, involving another milestone and another infusion of capital.

This staged decision approach should be familiar to anyone in new product development, where the *stage-gate system* of review and funding is widely used. The stage-gate system was developed by Robert Cooper in the late 1980s.[2] It is an alternating series of development stages and assessment gates that aims for early elimination of weak ideas and faster time to market for potential winners. These stages and gates control events from the initial idea all the way to commercialization.

FIGURE 7-2

Staged decision approach

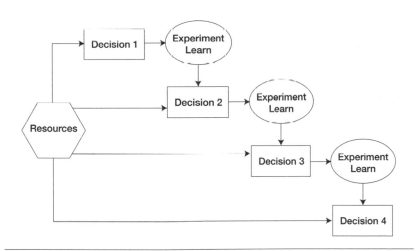

Figure 7–3 is a generic representation of that system. Here's how it works in practice:

- **Stages.** Stages are phases of the process in which development work is done. For example, a system would have stages for developing the raw idea, technical specifications, a prototype, and so forth. Commercialization is the final stage.

- **Gates.** Gates are decision checkpoints where people with expertise and the authority to allocate resources determine whether the project should be killed, sent back for more development, or advanced to the next development stage. Gates can be used at various points to determine strategic fit, whether the project passes technical and financial hurdles, whether it's ready for testing or launch, and so forth.

Both staged approaches shown here have proven their worth in limiting the risks involved in major decisions made under uncertainty. In both approaches the method is practical and simple: take small steps, evaluate your position, and gather additional information before you take a further step.

FIGURE 7-3

A stage-gate system

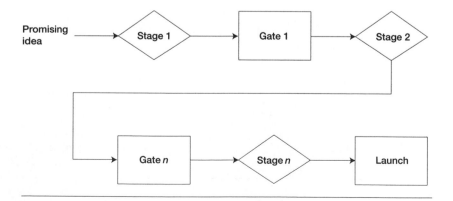

Be Prepared for the Worst

The savvy decision maker recognizes uncertainty and takes steps to reduce it to the extent that is possible and practical. But this decision maker does one more thing: he prepares for the worst. Preparing for a bad outcome begins with making a list of the specific things that could go wrong in a decision. Each item on the list should then provoke this question: "How will we respond if this happens?" The response should take the form of a contingency plan that aims to limit the damage and, hopefully, help the company recover from the bad outcome.

The Harvard Business Essentials series Web site has a handy checklist that you and your colleagues can use in brainstorming "The Ten Worst Things That Could Happen List." You can find a copy in appendix A of this book, or if you want to download it without charge, go to the series Web site: www.elearning.hbsp.org/ businesstools. And while you're there, help yourself to other tools that will help you in your work.

Chances are that you have many opportunities to reduce the key uncertainties (risks) involved with your decisions. Take a minute to think about the most recent decisions you have made. What were the key uncertainties—the ones that could have hurt you the most? Did you have practical opportunities to reduce those uncertainties by seeking more information or through any of the other means just described? If you passed up these opportunities, be sure to consider them the next time you make an important decision.

When to Trust Your Gut

Do you ever find yourself making decisions based on intuition, perhaps because a decision is required quickly, before relevant facts can be gathered and analyzed? Alternatively, do you ever find yourself saying, "Everything seems to add up, but I have a bad feeling about the choice we're about to make. Maybe we should hold off." If you do, you're in good company. Research indicates that 45 percent of executives rely on their intuition rather than on facts in running their businesses. And some have been extremely successful. Consider these examples:

- One of the founders of Sun Microsystems saw an early demonstration of a search engine developed by two graduate students. He invested $100,000 on the spot in what would become Google.

- Michael Eisner heard a pitch for a new TV show with the unlikely name *Who Wants to Be a Millionaire?* Something told him that it would be a winner, and he made a commitment to fund it.

- At the end of World War II in 1945, many share prices on the New York Stock Exchange were still far behind their 1929 peaks. Nor did the future look particularly bright. Yet John Templeton borrowed some money and bought a handful of shares of every stock listed on the exchange. That investment made a huge profit in the years that followed.

- Decades later, financier George Soros made a fortune by following his hunch that the currency markets were approaching a major shift.

Intuition, the mental process of assessing situations and forming conclusions without the intervention of factual information or analysis, appears to become more important as a person deals with complex decisions in which uncertainties and ambiguities are greatest. As Alden M. Hayashi told readers of *Harvard Business Review* in 2001, "The consensus is that the higher up on the corporate ladder people climb, the more they'll need well-honed business instincts. In other words, intuition is one of the X factors that separate the men from the boys."[3] According to Hayashi, the executives he interviewed on the subject variously use the terms "professional judgment," "intuition," "gut instinct," "inner voice," and "hunch" in referring to this decision-making tool, which he concedes may be more appropriate for decisions involving strategy, human resources, and product develop-ment than for others, such as production and finance.

What we call intuition is based on memories, pattern recogni-tion, accumulated experience, conditioning, and long-held per-sonal biases. How far should we go in trusting it? Certainly we know about the successes of intuition-based decisions, such as the four cited earlier. They make for great and memorable stories. Even luck plays a role in success (see "Catching the Zeitgeist in Holly-wood"). But we hear much less about failures, because their perpe-trators don't like to talk about them. Indeed, no experts in the field of decision making recommend reliance on intuition alone. Intu-ition is too subject to biases and to our tendency to see analogies where they don't exist. As one author, Eric Bonabeau, put it, "Any-one who thinks that intuition is a substitute for reason is indulging in a risky delusion. Detached from rigorous analysis, intuition is a fickle and undependable guide—it is as likely to lead to disaster as to success."[4]

Bonabeau, Hayashi, and others who have studied this issue agree that intuition can be useful, but only insofar as it works in tandem with rational analysis. In other words, the right side of the brain, which houses our intuitive power, must collaborate with the left side, the source of logic and analytical power. Kim Wallace, chair-man of Wallace and Washburn, a Boston-based marketing research and consultancy firm, discovered this for himself many years ago. "The key to making a decision," Wallace told us in early 2005, "is to delay the decision until it makes logical sense *and* it feels right. The two sides of the brains must agree. If they don't, delay the decision. Get more input from more sources until it eventually lines up on both logical and intuitive perspectives. This sounds very simple, and it is. But I have never made a bad decision using this process."[5]

Uncertainty is the constant companion of decision makers and a source of business risk. You will never eliminate it, but you can un-derstand it and take steps to reduce it. But uncertainty isn't the only challenge you face. There are also human factors to consider, as dis-cussed in chapter 8.

Catching the Zeitgeist in Hollywood

Decision makers must rely on their instincts to some extent, and even more so in the motion picture business. Movie executives must contend with finicky audiences, temperamental box-office stars, heavyweight producers, and multimillion-dollar production costs. Knowing how audiences will respond to a script is anyone's guess—or should we say, anyone's informed guess.

Sherry Lansing, chairperson of Paramount Pictures Group, has created many of Hollywood's blockbusters, including *Braveheart*, *Forrest Gump*, and *Titantic,* one of the largest-grossing films in history. With millions at stake and a high level of uncertainty, what's her approach to making decisions? As she described in an October 2004 interview with *Time*, Lansing combines data, intuition, and judgment about the people who will head the project. "I read all the market research and use it as a tool," she said. "But movies are an art form. You have to look into the eyes of a filmmaker and an executive and see their passion." She also hopes for luck. "Luck is needed in nearly every business, but even more so in this one, where you have to catch the zeitgeist, and the zeitgeist moves so quickly."[a]

[a] Jeffrey Ressner, "The Art of Betting $100," *Time*, October 4, 2004, 62–63.

Summing Up

- When a decision involves a high level of uncertainty, try this three-step approach: (1) identify the areas of uncertainty, (2) determine which uncertainties could have the greatest impact on the outcome of your decision, and (3) reduce key uncertainties to the extent that you have the time and resources to do so.

- As you gather estimates of uncertain future outcomes, avoid point estimates. These are bound to be wrong. Instead, try to estimate a range of likely outcomes.

- In estimating the probability of a particular outcome, don't rely solely on your own judgment. Instead, enlist the views of the most experienced and knowledgeable people.

- Narrowing time gaps, building to order, adopting risk-limiting tactics, and making staged decisions are four ways to manage the risks in decisions.

- Intuition is the mental process of assessing situations and forming conclusions without the intervention of factual information or analysis.

- Intuition can be useful when it works in tandem with rational analysis.

Human Foibles

*How to Counter Tendencies That
Can Ambush Your Decision*

Key Topics Covered in This Chapter

- *How to avoid the anchoring trap*

- *How to keep overconfidence from
  leading you to a bad decision*

- *Why sunk costs should not affect
  decisions about the future*

- *Avoiding the bias of confirming evidence*

- *How to avoid making a false analogy*

I N THE OLD TELEVISION series *Star Trek*, Spock, the super-rational, emotionless Vulcan, was always puzzled by the behavior of his human companions. To Spock, Captain Kirk and other crew members seemed to be ruled by their feelings. Instead of making perfectly logical decisions—as a computerlike Vulcan would—the humans aboard the *Enterprise* were often governed by fear, anger, self-pity, pride, self-deception, ambition, and overconfidence. Spock must have wondered how the human race had managed to survive.

Previous chapters have presented a logical, rational process for making decisions. Spock would surely recommend it. This process, however, is nothing more than a tool in the hands of people who operate with emotions and foibles. Just as an automobile is a utilitarian piece of machinery, its usefulness is undermined when the person at the wheel is reckless, aggressive, or inattentive. Similarly, the utility of our decision process can be subverted by the individual or group using it.

This chapter describes a number of decision traps: human behaviors that can come between you and an effective decision. The list is by no means exhaustive, but it hits the main ones. Watch for them the next time you're faced with making a decision.

Anchoring and Adjustment

Negotiation experts use the term *anchoring* to refer to a tactic that attempts to establish an initial position around which negotiations will take place. In the right circumstances, the first person to put a price on the table establishes a psychological anchor point around which subsequent discussion and counteroffers generally revolve.

For example, suppose you list your house for sale for $500,000. Most interested buyers will respond to that price. "We'll offer $475,000," says one. Another says, "I'll offer $470,000 if the seller will first repair the water damage in the cellar." Studies have shown that the outcomes of negotiations often correlate with initial anchor points.

In their book *Smart Choices,* John Hammond III, Ralph Keeney, and Howard Raiffa describe two questions they have used to study what they call the anchor trap. Answer them for yourself:

1. Is the population of Turkey greater than 35 million?

2. What's your best estimate of Turkey's population?

How did you answer these questions? Was your answer to question 2 influenced by the number in question 1? These authors find that the first question anchors the response to the second question. "Over the years," they write, "we've posed these questions to many groups of people. In half the cases we use 35 million in the first question; in the other half we use 100 million. Without fail, the answers to the second question increase by many millions when the larger figure is used in the first question."[1]

Anchoring also creeps into decision making, sometimes deliberately. An advocate for a particular course may, for example, submit a sales forecast favorable to her proposal:

Looking out over the first three-year life of this new product on the market, we have forecast the following annual net revenues:

2007: $2.4 million

2008: $3.5 million

2009: $4.9 million

If members of the decision team sense what their colleague is doing in this maneuver, they will quickly dismiss these revenue figures before they anchor the discussion:

> *It's premature to be forecasting sales at this early point. Let's first talk about the target market and the competition.*

Less astute team members might go for the bait, happy to have tangible, quantitative measures on the table. They might quibble with the forecast numbers, but they will make adjustments in reference to the initial anchors.

We all respond to anchors in our daily lives, usually without noticing. For example, when we're asked to develop a department expense budget, our starting point is almost always last year's budget. It's a convenient anchor point. And it may be a valid baseline against which to make adjustments, especially if the department will have the same number of personnel and the same set of duties. Otherwise, it can present an anchor trap.

An Antidote to Anchoring and Adjustment

Whether or not it's done deliberately, anchoring can lead you into a bad decision. Here are some measures you can take to avoid the anchor trap:

- Recognize it when you see it. Remember that some people try to manipulate the thinking of others by using an initial set of numbers.

- Immunize yourself against an anchor. Do your homework on the issue, and form your own thoughts *before* any numbers are placed on the table. This will make you less susceptible to someone else's anchor.

- Ask for and challenge the assumptions underlying any anchor. If someone throws down a number, approach it as a hypothesis. "How did you arrive at this estimate?" is a fair question to ask. "What were the assumptions in your calculation?" Make the person lay out a logical case for his position.

- Don't plant anchors when you seek independent viewpoints. Independent viewpoints bring strength to the decision-making process, so when you speak with colleagues and consultants, avoid making statements like this one: "I think this product could sell between 20,000 and 30,000 units each year in the adult men's market. What do you think?" Instead, keep mum and let others present their own thoughts.

Overconfidence

Overconfidence in one's capabilities to forecast the future, assess risks, control events, and anticipate others' actions is one of the greatest and most common decision-making foibles. As Dan Lovallo and Daniel Kahneman told readers of the *Harvard Business Review,* business leaders unconsciously exaggerate their personal abilities and management skills. Their self-confidence encourages them to assume that they'll be able to control the outcomes of difficult situations. Consequently, they are likely to make decisions "based on delusional optimism rather than on a rational weighing of gains, losses, and probabilities. They overestimate benefits and underestimate costs . . . As a result, managers pursue initiatives that are unlikely to come in on budget or on time—or to ever deliver the expected returns."[2]

Vincent Barabba observed this when he first went to work at General Motors in 1988. As he and colleagues attempted to reform the giant automaker's decision process, he was struck by the optimism of sales and cost forecasts, few of which could be supported by rigorous analysis.[3]

This tendency of executives to be overconfident and optimistic may explain why, despite the well-known fact that mergers and acquisitions fail to produce desired results almost 75 percent of the time, companies by the thousands take the M&A route every year. It also explains why, despite the woeful record of new product introductions, managers express confidence in the many new products they will put into the mill each year.

Overconfidence leads us to believe that things will turn out as we wish, and it encourages us to disregard warning signs of impending trouble, as in the following cautionary tale.

During the early months of 1942, Japan's naval commanders were in high spirits. They were, as one historian put it, awash in self-adulation. And why not? Their attack on the U.S. base at Pearl Harbor had exceeded all expectations. So had subsequent ground and sea actions in the Philippines and Indochina.

Brimming with confidence, they began planning their next strategic moves: establishing a base in the Aleutian Islands, capturing Midway Island, and drawing the remnants of the U.S. Navy into an ambush on the high seas. As part of their planning, the top fleet commanders and their staffs conducted tabletop simulations. One participant, aviation commander Mitsuo Fuchida, later described the flawless results of those simulations, but also the presiding officer's tendency to bend the rules when things went badly for his side. "A situation developed in which [our carrier force] underwent a bombing attack by enemy land-based aircraft while its own planes were off attacking Midway," Fuchida wrote. "In accordance with the rules [dice were cast] to determine the bombing results, it was ruled that there had been nine enemy hits on the Japanese carriers. Both Akagi and Kaga were listed as sunk. Admiral Ugaki, however, arbitrarily reduced the number of enemy hits to three, which resulted in Kaga still being sunk but Akagi only slightly damaged . . . even this revised ruling was subsequently cancelled, and Kaga reappeared."[4]

Five weeks later, the simulated events unfolded at the pivotal Battle of Midway. In the tangled events of the day, one of the critical developments of the simulation actually occurred: the four carriers in the Japanese task force were attacked by enemy aircraft while their planes were either returning from action over Midway or being refueled on the decks. Each was repeatedly hit, as suggested by the simulation. But this time, there was no presiding officer to overturn the results. Akagi, Kaga, and the two other carriers went down with their planes and crews.

This same type of overconfidence afflicts business planners and decision makers. One need only read stock research reports from the heyday of the dot-com boom to recognize how the judgment of normally straitlaced, left-brained security analysts was impaired by overconfidence and the madness of crowds. "Star" analysts who recommended purchases of eBay, Amazon.com, Priceline.com, and dozens of other skyrocketing stocks seemed to have the Midas touch.

Their mistake, as we understand from hindsight, was to confuse a bullish stock market with their own forecasting brilliance. They compounded this error as stock prices lost all touch with real value. Although traditional valuation methods screamed, "These stocks are overpriced!" emboldened analysts simply concocted new yardsticks of value, such as "market value per customer" and "market value per Web page viewer" to explain why these securities represented good value—and still had plenty of upside. As stock analysts told their critics at the time, the world had changed; the old measures of share value no longer applied.

You may recall how these stock gurus were humbled in the great market tumble that began in January 2000. Similar tales can be found in the annals of M&A. One example is Quaker Oats Company's $2 billion bid to acquire the Snapple beverage line, which it divested two years later for a mere $300 million. The executive team's overconfidence in its ability to expand Snapple's sales was at the heart of this costly failure.

Although we usually celebrate confidence and optimism as business virtues and as qualities without which we cannot lead or manage, there is substantial evidence that confidence and optimism often are not justified by the facts. In his award-winning book *The Psychology of Judgment and Decision Making,* Scott Plous describes a test administered to 3,500 people, who were asked to (1) answer certain questions and (2) indicate their level of confidence in each answer. According to Plous, "People's confidence ratings were virtually unrelated to their accuracy (the average correlations between confidence and accuracy for each respondent was only [0.08], very close to zero). On the whole, people who got nine or ten items correct were no more confident than less successful respondents, and highly confident respondents scored about the same as less confident respondents."[5] This is merely one test. Plous concludes that in most studies, "average confidence levels do not exceed accuracy by more than ten to twenty percent."[6] Thus, a normal level of confidence may not cause a decision maker to veer too far off course. But it should set off alarm bells when your confidence is immense or based heavily on past success.

Put a Damper on Overconfidence

Has unsupportable confidence crept into your planning and decision making? Here are some suggestions for keeping it in check:

- Look for cases of extreme confidence. This is where the danger is greatest. When you find one of these cases, call a time-out. Bring in people who have a scientific sense of skepticism, and ask them to participate in examining the situation.

- Talk with the superconfident decision maker. Ask him to explain what makes him so confident, and then examine each assumption, belief, or piece of evidence.

- Ask the superconfident decision maker to change roles and act as an advocate of an opposing viewpoint.

Apply Reference Class Forecasting

One of the most common symptoms of overconfidence and undue optimism is found in the forecasts that decision makers are willing to accept. Optimistic managers sometimes fall in love with projects, and when they do they are prone to believe that those projects will enjoy much greater success than have similar past projects. Consider this case:

> A book publisher had a group of inexperienced acquisition editors. Before they could offer a contract to a prospective author, they were required to run the numbers—that is, estimate the profitability of the book being considered. The starting point was to forecast a title's first-year unit sales through retail and wholesale channels. More than any other factor—manufacturing costs and the like—unit sales were the

most uncertain and *the most critical to profitability. Nevertheless, a forecast had to be made.*

The CFO, who had recently joined the company from a different industry, had no way of knowing whether the editors' forecasts were reasonable. So he did some checking. He looked back over the first-year unit sales of previously published books in key subject areas; he then compared the actual results to the forecasts made for those same books. This back-checking produced a startling discovery: some 84 percent of the company's past publications had never gotten close to their first-year forecasts. Among books on finance, for example, he found that editors had routinely forecast first-year average sales of seven thousand units. In reality, the average for books in that subject category was only about forty-five hundred units.

Unduly optimistic editors in this case were treating *each* of their projects as well above average. This type of behavior is not uncommon. Authors Dan Lovallo and Daniel Kahneman have suggested a method for counteracting this problem: *reference class forecasting*. This method requires forecasters to do the following:

1. Identify a reference class of analogous past projects whose outcomes are known.

2. Determine the distribution of outcomes for those projects along a continuum, from high to low.

3. Place the project being considered at an appropriate point along that distribution.[7]

The result is usually a more realistic forecast, because you will see in an instant whether you are predicting an outcome in the high end of the range.

In our example, an editor who wanted to use reference class forecasting to make a reasonable first-year unit sales estimate for a new book on, say, human resource management would do the following. First, she would identify a reference class of analogous past projects—in this case, previously published books on HR management. She would then determine the distribution of outcomes for those books by consulting the sales data.

Selecting the reference class is important and should be done with care. Let's say that the company had published six books in HR management over the past few years. Their first-year unit sales, arrayed by size, were as follows:

A. 3,800

B. 4,650

C. 6,100

D. 6,950

E. 8,200

F. 8,800

The range here is 3,800 on the low end and 8,800 on the high end. The average first-year unit sales for this reference class is 6,417, and the distribution around the average is fairly normal—that is, we don't have a bunch of very low sales and another bunch of extremely high ones.

Finally, the editor would try to place the HR book she hoped to publish at an appropriate point within that distribution. One way to do that would be to simply use the average figure for the reference class—6,417—as the estimate. A more thoughtful approach would be to make adjustments based on the unique qualities of the new book. For example, the editor might say, "Well, this new book is somewhat similar to book D; it aims for the same market of readers and is on a complementary subject." She would then consider other factors in adjusting her forecast higher or lower than book D's. "I think we can expect more sales from this new book because the author is much better known than the author of book D, and his consulting firm is planning to hire a publicist and do other marketing. So I'll estimate 8,000 copies for the first year it's in print."

Obviously, there's still some room for optimistic bias to creep in, so others might challenge the editor's reasons for giving her new book an above-average sales forecast. As you've probably noticed, there's a mix of art and science in this reference class forecasting method. It's imperfect, but it's still an effective way of dealing with uncertainty and the risk of relying on some people's natural optimism.

Sunk Costs

In the language of economics, *sunk costs* are investments of time or money that cannot be recovered. Sunk costs are about the past, but people sometimes make the mistake of allowing sunk costs to influence decisions about the future. Consider this example:

> Phil has paid $50 for a ticket to a concert featuring his favorite blue-grass band. Two hours before the concert begins, his boss calls to say that the board of directors meeting has just ended and they are going out to dinner. "I'd like you to join us," says the boss. "This is a great opportunity for you to get to know the board members and vice versa."
>
> "Wow," Phil thinks. "Face time with the board! This could really help my career." But being naive, he declines because he has already invested $50 in a concert ticket. His rationale? "I'd hate to waste that money."

In this example, the $50 was out the window whether or not Phil used his ticket. Yet he allowed that sunk cost to dictate another decision that clearly had high payoff potential.

Decision makers commit this mistake frequently—sometimes because they fail to recognize that the sunk cost cannot be recouped, but more often because it's personally painful to take the loss and move on. Why? It's because moving on would reflect badly on the initial decision. This is why the executive who championed your company's failed marketing plan continues to defend it when the need for change is apparent to everyone else. "We need to give the strategy more time," the executive argues.

The sunk cost foible also explains why many managers are slow in facing up to poor hiring decisions. They've hired someone and invested in his training, but he clearly has not been doing the job despite counseling and coaching. Instead of facing up to this bad hiring decision, managers usually make another poor decision: to invest still more time in training and coaching, hoping for a turnaround.

Two executives interviewed for this book pointed to bad hiring decisions as the most difficult to rectify. "The most difficult decision for me is when to give up on a person and get rid of him," said one. "I always wait way too long to do that." "Generally, I think the most challenging decision to make is when to pull the plug," said another. "Around here we always take too long. We are always hopeful that things will improve."

Neutralizing the Sunk Cost Bias

Does your company have a case of the sunk cost problem? Like most decision biases, the best antidote is to expose it. Don't allow it to lurk in the background. Here's how:

- Help people recognize sunk costs that are influencing their current decisions.

- Explain that everyone makes mistakes—hiring the wrong person, backing the wrong strategy, and so forth. These are usually forgivable. What's not forgivable is allowing one mistake to cause another.

- If possible, don't staff your decision team with people who have sunk cost biases.

The Confirming–Evidence Bias

Have you ever found yourself actively seeking evidence to support your point of view, while discounting or dismissing contrary evidence? If you have, take comfort in the fact that many people do. It's a very natural behavior.

If you doubt that, watch how people operate when highly contentious issues are brought to the councils of management. For example, a marketing manager, keen on carving out a new sales territory, will hunt down all the data that supports her idea, but none of the reasons for not doing it. Sometimes this bias is deliberate. "My old boss did this all the time," one manager we interviewed told us.

"She always thought that she, more than anyone else, knew what was best for the company. And she'd ask us to gather evidence to support her view. Any information that conflicted with or contradicted that view was, in her opinion, simply wrong and was discarded."

Hammond, Keeney, and Raiffa call this the *confirming-evidence bias*. This bias, they say, "not only affects where we go to collect evidence but also how we interpret the evidence we do receive, leading us to give too much weight to supporting information and too little to conflicting information."[8]

Be Evenhanded

As with other biases, the best defense against the confirming-evidence bias is self-awareness. Try to stand outside yourself for a moment and ask whether you are being honest in how you gather and interpret information. If someone on your decision team is a victim of this bias—or is using it deliberately—make it your job to represent the opposing view. For example, if the marketing manager is making a case for creating a new sales territory, find whatever information you can to support *not* doing so.

Enlist Objective Data Gatherers

If you have the personnel to handle it, ask a competent and respected staff person—someone with no personal interest in the decision—to gather and present all the relevant facts to the management team. Divide these facts into those that support the proposal and those that do not.

False Analogies

Experience is a useful form of learning. We would be adrift without it. Having slipped and tumbled on one or two icy sidewalks, we know to approach them with caution. Experience also guides us in our work and our decisions. We learn to recognize patterns in situations and associate them with specific outcomes—both good and bad. Icy sidewalk. Falling. Pain.

> *Janice, a product line manager, has twice used discount coupons to promote the sales of newly introduced packaged cake mixes in grocery stores. Other product managers routinely use this promotional gimmick, and with good results. In both instances Janice expected sales to increase by 20 percent. But she was disappointed. Sales increased by only 5 to 10 percent, barely enough to cover the cost of the promotion. These two experiences temper Janice's enthusiasm for this marketing tactic and alter her expectations of its usefulness.*

We carry these patterns and outcomes with us and routinely draw on them as we encounter new and similar situations. When two or more things in a new situation match what we have experienced in the past, we might infer that they will probably match in other respects. In effect, we form an *analogy* that guides our thinking—and our decisions.

Analogies are among the mental tools we use to bridge the gap between what we've experienced in the past and the situations we face now. Indeed, they are part of the intuition, or gut instinct, on which many experienced managers rely for guidance in situations of uncertainty. Used judiciously, analogies can be useful. As historian Joseph Strayer once put it, "There will always be familiar elements in a new situation that will aid us in making decisions and in judging what the results of those decisions will be. The wider and deeper our experience, the greater our chances of recognizing those familiar elements."[9]

More than a few major decisions have been triggered by analogies. When communist North Korea invaded its southern neighbor in 1950, U.S. President Harry S. Truman immediately saw an analogy between that event and what he had experienced as a younger man. "In my generation," he wrote, "this was not the first occasion when the strong had attacked the weak. I recalled some earlier instances: Manchuria, Ethiopia, Austria. I remembered how each time that the democracies failed to act it had encouraged the aggressors to keep going. Communism was acting in Korea just as Hitler, Mussolini, and the Japanese had acted . . . years earlier."[10]

But unless we are careful, analogies can trick us into making very bad and costly decisions. In many respects this is what befell a later U.S. president, Lyndon Johnson, when he was confronted with conflict in Vietnam. Like Truman, Johnson and his advisers had vivid memories of totalitarian aggression in the run-up to World War II. Aggression by the North Koreans reinforced those memories. By seeing fighting in Vietnam as more of the same, and not as an anti-colonial movement with strong indigenous support, Johnson created and acted on a false analogy.

Businesspeople are equally vulnerable to false analogies. Consider our hypothetical case of Janice, the marketer:

> *After three years as a product line manager for a chain of supermarkets, Janice has become marketing manager for a regional chain of clothing boutiques. The chain's management team is new and inexperienced in the use of promotional methods, and yet they are eager to use some form of promotion to generate interest in their new fall collection. The team naturally looks to Janice for advice.*
>
> *"I was wondering if a discount coupon in local newspapers—say, $10 off the price of a $100 purchase—would be a good way to get people into the stores during the first week or two of the fall fashion season," says Helen, the CEO.*
>
> *Janice's mind returns to her disappointing experience in introducing the cake mix product. It seems to be an analogous situation: trying to generate customer interest in a newly introduced product by using discount coupons. True, apparel is not cake mix, she thinks, but customers are customers and are likely to respond in the same way. "I'm not favorable to this type of promotion," she tells the CEO. "My experience is that you will generate more sales activity but will give most of it back in discounts."*

Steer Clear of False Analogies

Clearly, our propensity to form analogies can help guide our decisions in situations of uncertainty. But it can also trick us, as it may have tricked Janice. So how can we steer clear of false analogies?

The best advice on making the most of analogy can be found in *Thinking in Time: The Uses of History for Decision Makers* by Richard Neustadt and Ernest May, then senior professors at Harvard's Kennedy School of Government.[11] Neustadt and May developed a methodology they hoped would help Kennedy School students—the next generation of government and military policy makers—steer clear of false analogies. Their methodology is based on five questions:

1. What is known about the situation?

2. What is unclear?

3. What is presumed?

4. What are the likenesses to past events?

5. What are the differences?

Each of these questions should be the basis for inquiry and reflection. And each should be answered. If you do this you'll be less likely to form and fall victim to a false analogy.

We've examined a number of human foibles that creep into the decision-making process—and always for the worse. Have you observed any in your company's decisions? Awareness of these foibles is the best antidote.

But individual biases and delusion are not the only threats to making good decisions. There are also organizational foibles to consider, the subject of chapter 9.

Summing Up

- Anchoring establishes an initial position around which subsequent negotiations and discussion often take place. In the right circumstances, the first person to put a price on the table establishes a psychological anchor point.

- Executives are often overconfident about their ability to forecast the future, assess risks, control events, and anticipate actions by others. This overconfidence often leads them to make decision errors. One way to counteract the overconfident decision maker is to have another person challenge his position and advocate an opposing view.

- Reference class forecasting is another antidote to misplaced confidence. It requires decision makers to methodically position their projects in a continuum of similar projects whose outcomes are known.

- Sunk costs are past investments of time or money that cannot be recovered. Decision makers should not allow sunk costs to influence their decisions about the future.

- The confirming-evidence bias encourages decision makers to seek out and rely on information that confirms their existing beliefs and to discount or ignore nonconfirming evidence.

- Analogies are among the mental tools we use to bridge the gap between what we've experienced and the situations we face now. Used judiciously, analogies are useful. However, false analogies can lead us to make bad decisions.

Organizational Traps

The Madness—and the Wisdom—of Crowds

Key Topics Covered in This Chapter

- *The impact of social influences on decision makers*

- *Groupthink and how to combat it*

- *The problem of excessive optimism*

- *When groups make better decisions than individuals*

I N 1841, SCOTSMAN CHARLES Mackay published *Extraordinary Popular Delusions and the Madness of Crowds,* a book containing a loosely connected series of historical episodes in which the author described how otherwise sober people succumbed to mass hysteria that caused them to lose all semblance of good judgment and common sense. Mackay's tales include the Crusades, the great land speculation of the South Sea Bubble, the seventeenth-century "tulipomania" (in which Dutch citizens bid up the price of tulip bulbs to incredible levels), the witch manias, and others. In each instance, the infectious character of group behavior spread, carrying along people who should have known better.

Mackay described group behavior at its worst. Individuals are generally more sober and judicious. Nevertheless, what goes on in business—including decision making—is swayed by the influence of the group. This chapter examines several ways in which social and group influences can infect a logical decision process, producing undesirable outcomes. And like chapter 8, it offers practical suggestions for avoiding them.

Social Influences

There is little doubt that individuals within a group (within a decision team, a business unit, a company) are subject to the influences of those around them, even when they have the power to ignore them in making a final decision. As psychologist Scott Plous has stated, "Because people are social by nature, their judgments and decisions are subject to social influences. Even when decision makers operate alone, they often tailor their behavior in anticipation of how it will be evaluated by others. Consequently, any comprehensive account of judgment and decision making must include social factors."[1]

Some decision makers are influenced by a desire to

- please others

- avoid conflict

- avoid being out of step with others

- be seen as part of the group

- avoid the criticism that follows an unpopular decision

How susceptible are you and your colleagues to these influences? Are any of them shaping your business decisions?

The power of social influence on individual decisions was strikingly demonstrated in an experiment conducted in 1951 by Solomon Asch. A pioneer in social psychology, Asch enlisted college students to participate in what appeared to be a scientific experiment designed to measure visual perception. The volunteer sat around a table with seven strangers. An experimenter then placed two cards similar to those in figure 9-1 in front of each subject. She then asked the participants to indicate, one following another, which of the three lines on the right card matched the length of the line on the left card. This process was repeated several times with different cards.

What the volunteer did not know was that the others at the table were not volunteers but shills—associates of the experimenter—and each was following a script. The true volunteer was, by design, the

FIGURE 9-1

Asch's cards

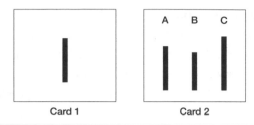

| Card 1 | Card 2 |

last to be asked, "Which line on card 2 is the same length as the line on card 1?" As the last to respond, the volunteer had an opportunity to consider how each of the others had answered. Would he be influenced by those answers? That was the question Asch's experiment hoped to answer.

During several rounds of the experiment, the shills unanimously gave an answer that no one with normal perception would give. They said, for example, that line B matched the line in card 1. The volunteer was then asked for his answer.

How would you answer if everyone else in the room had already identified B as the correct answer? Would you trust the evidence of your own eyes, or would you be swayed by the unanimous judgment of the group?

Asch found that thirty-seven of his fifty volunteer subjects conformed to the majority opinion at least once, and fourteen of them conformed on more than six of the twelve repetitions of the experiment. When faced with a wrong but unanimous vote by the other group members, the average subject conformed on four of the twelve trials.[2]

Asch repeated his experiment in different settings and with variations. These produced two important findings:

- Interviewed later, most subjects said that they didn't believe the answers they gave but went along with the group out of a fear of being ridiculed or being perceived as "peculiar." They wanted to be liked and accepted by the group.

- A few subjects claimed that they really believed that the answers of the experimenter's confederates were correct.

- The number of conforming subjects dropped dramatically when they had an "ally" in the group. Asch occasionally had one of his confederates give the right answer. Having even one ally in the group was enough encouragement for conformity to drop like a rock.

The implications of Asch's findings for business decision makers are obvious and troubling. Not wanting to be viewed as out of step with their colleagues, some people will put their own opinions aside and fall in line with the majority. We can speculate that this is doubly true when there are substantial power differences between people on a decision-making team.

This tendency to conform has two negative effects:

- The group is deprived of a dissenting view.

- The group's confidence in its view is bound to rise.

Neither of these effects contributes to sound decision making.

Reducing Conformity

You can reduce the perils of conformity by altering group decision-making processes. One approach is to ask each participant to privately write down her judgment *before* the views of other participants are known. Have a facilitator act as receiver and keeper of those written views.

Another approach is to insist that the high-ranking people on the decision team be the last to express their views. In that way, other people will not be intimidated and will get their true viewpoints on the table.

Groupthink

Every decision-making team is endangered by an organization foible known as *groupthink*. And the more close-knit the team is, the higher the risk. The late Irving Janus, the Yale psychologist who coined the term, defined groupthink as a mode of thinking found in cohesive in-groups. The zeal for unanimity in these groups overrides any realistic appraisal of alternative actions.

Groupthink is the result of convergence of thinking around a norm and is a potential side effect of strong team identity. Unfortunately, that convergence is driven less by objectivity than by social psychological pressures. When all members identify strongly with the team, they may highlight similarities (while suppressing differences) and strive to agree with each other. This can engender cooperation, a good thing, but also can inadvertently curtail critical thinking and debate, a very bad thing. The impulse for agreement and unity in these situations takes priority over objectivity.

Social psychologists have long observed that opinions within groups tend to converge as group members become aware of the opinions of their peers. For example, when polled separately about their forecasts of future interest rates, economists generally produce a broad range of rates. After they learn what their peers are thinking, however, the range miraculously narrows, with most forecasts clustering close to the mean. This convergence is explained by the reluctance of individuals—perhaps due to a lack of self-confidence—to make forecasts that are substantially out of step with the forecasts of others. Perhaps you've observed the same phenomenon in group meetings you've attended.

Convergence of opinion is important for decision-making teams, especially with respect to goals, the ways decisions should be made, and the norms of group behavior. It's difficult for a group to function effectively if it lacks consensus on these issues. But convergence that escalates to groupthink is dangerous. Diversity of views gives way to homogeneity, which creates an illusion of certitude. Those who "think otherwise" may even be reeducated or pushed out.

Here are some symptoms of groupthink:

- Group members hold an illusion of invulnerability.

- Leaders are insulated (protected) from contradictory evidence.

- Members accept confirming data and reject data that fails to fit with their views (the confirming-evidence bias discussed in chapter 8).

- Alternatives are not considered.

- Individuals whose views are out of step with the majority are discounted or demonized.

- The same people who develop plans are asked to critique them.

How to Avoid Groupthink

Do you recognize any of these symptoms in your decision team? If you do, leaders and members must take steps to welcome a diversity of thoughtful ideas. One way to do this is to appoint a respected and qualified person to the role of devil's advocate. This person should have a charter: to challenge the assumptions and conclusions of the majority. He will also represent dissenting views and insist that other members deal with facts and ideas that conflict with their own.

Rewarding Optimists and Punishing Pessimists

Another group influence is found in the culture of some organizations. These organizations emphasize and reward optimism and penalize pessimism. They pride themselves on their "can-do" spirit and maintain that no challenge is too great. Leaders who support this culture remind employees, "When the going gets tough, the tough get going." The CEO periodically issues challenging stretch goals with the encouragement that "there's nothing you cannot do if you put your mind to it."

Optimism is a virtue for individuals and organizations. Indeed, it is difficult to imagine human progress without it. Optimism, however, has a dark side when it loses touch with reality. Decision makers smitten by the can-do spirit may accept imprudent levels of risk and agree to unrealistic forecasts; speaking against these excesses may be impolitic and limit one's career. To argue for greater prudence, to say, "I don't think we can achieve these numbers," may even be taken as a sign of disloyalty: "If you can't make those numbers, Ms. Quimby, I'll find someone who can."

The most dangerous aspect of excessive optimism for an organization is the tendency to promote optimists and marginalize people labeled as pessimists. This tendency ensures that the optimists will eventually control all decisions, making a bad situation worse. Dan Lovallo and Daniel Kahneman observe the following in their article "Delusions of Success":

> *The bearers of bad news tend to become pariahs, shunned and ignored by other employees. When pessimistic opinions are suppressed, while optimistic ones are rewarded, an organization's ability to think critically is undermined. The optimistic biases of individual employees become mutually reinforcing, and unrealistic views of the future are validated by the group.*[3]

Promote Tempered Optimism

What is the role of optimism in your company's culture? Do people appreciate the difference between being foolhardy and realistic optimism? The top leadership must understand that difference and must rid the organization's culture of the former. Few things are as destructive to morale as taking on a superhuman task and then failing to deliver.

Perhaps the best antidote to intemperate optimism is to conduct an objective analysis of alternatives. For example, if one of the superoptimists suggests that acquiring a certain company will facilitate penetration of an adjacent geographic market, politely ask for empirical evidence to support that suggestion. In the absence of evidence, the person's proposal is nothing more than an untested and unexamined hypothesis. Your request for evidence is reasonable.

The reference class forecasting technique described in chapter 8 is another method for examining the factual basis of proposals that may be overly optimistic.

When Groups Make Better Decisions

Despite the periodic madness of crowds described by Charles Mackay and the more subtle influences that groups have over individuals, a group is usually more likely to make a better decision or find a better solution than is an individual acting alone. There is no denying the fact of individual genius. All the great works of symphonic music, for example, are the products of individual composers. There was no Mozart Collaborative. *Guernica* is not the work of a committee but of a single painter. *David Copperfield* did not emerge from the London Writers Forum but from the solitary labors of Charles Dickens. Nevertheless, many of the individual geniuses we recognize today benefited from feedback given by reviewers, editors, friends, and peers.

Despite notable individual achievements, groups are generally better than individuals when it comes to making decisions and solving problems. Simply putting the collective know-how and experience of three or four people on a problem raises the chance that someone in the group will know how to solve it. Alternatively, several individual group members may have partial solutions that, when combined, solve the entire problem.

In 2004, *New Yorker* financial writer James Surowiecki published a little book with the provocative title *The Wisdom of Crowds*, in which he reviewed the literature on this subject. He contends that the many are smarter than the few: "A large group of diverse individuals will come up with better and more robust forecasts and make more intelligent decisions than even the most skilled 'decision maker.'"[4]

Being familiar with the group biases that thwart sound decision making, Surowiecki wisely qualifies his faith in the wisdom of crowds by insisting on four conditions. They have the effect of minimizing group biases and making the most of having many minds address a problem.

1. **Diversity of opinion.** Each person in the group should have some "private information," that is, information not available to others. In this sense, diversity of opinion enriches the mix.

2. **Independence.** The opinions of group members should not be determined by those around them (for example, by their boss, who is participating in the decision).

3. **Decentralization.** As Surowiecki puts it, people should be able "to specialize and draw on local knowledge." In other words, decision makers should not be drawing from the same small body of information.

4. **Aggregation.** There should be a mechanism for converting individual judgments into a collective judgment—and a decision.[5] Elections, for example, are mechanisms for producing a collective judgment about politicians and their policies. Without elections, judgments would remain private and could not be acted on by the body politic.

It seems reasonable that a group that meets these four conditions would be positioned to make a good decision. The challenge is in meeting the conditions. It is difficult in a company setting, for example, to get true independence because the members of a group are bound to influence their colleagues. Just as Solomon Asch's unwitting volunteers had to listen to the judgments of others before they opened their mouths, all but one member of a decision team— the first to speak—will hear what others think before they render their own verdicts. Power differences between individuals within companies are also likely to undermine independent judgment. Still, Surowiecki's four conditions are worth considering as you assemble the members of a decision team.

Because we are social animals, our opinions and decisions are affected by those around us. Your job as an individual decision maker—or as the leader of a decision team—is to harness the wisdom of the group while keeping the group's corrosive influences at bay. It isn't easy, but your success will improve the odds of making an effective decision.

Summing Up

- We are social animals, and our judgments are influenced by those around us.

- The judgment of some decision makers is influenced by a desire to please others, to avoid conflict, to be in step with others or a part of the group, or to avoid post-decision criticism.

- Groupthink is a potential side effect of strong team identity. The highlighting of similarities in thinking and the suppression or avoidance of differences characterize groupthink.

- Be wary of undue optimism. Optimism is necessary for progress, but it must have a factual basis.

- Although groups are subject to "the madness of crowds," groups can make better decisions than individuals, according to James Surowiecki, when certain conditions prevail: a diversity of opinion, the independence of group members, decentralization, and the presence of a mechanism for converting individual judgments into a decision.

Toward a Smarter Organization

Getting Better at Making Decisions

Key Topics Covered in This Chapter

- *The virtue of making high-quality decisions*

- *A case example*

- *Six lessons*

- *What leaders should do*

- *Continual improvement in decision making*

T HE GOAL OF EVERY organization should be to improve the quality of its decisions. Achievement of that goal is its own reward. Can you imagine how your company's bottom line would improve if senior executive decisions improved by as little as 25 percent? One out of four costly mistakes—in filling top positions, in pricing products and services, in deal making, in strategy formulation—would be eliminated and replaced by a smart choice that improved effectiveness or made the enterprise more competitive. Employee energy, often wasted by poor executive decisions, would be directed toward activities that really create value.

Bad decisions by executives can never be eliminated because leaders live in an uncertain world, but replacing some bad decisions with good ones can make a huge difference in the fortunes of a business and its owners. Indeed, an investment in decision-making improvement may have a higher return than almost anything else a company can do, and for a simple reason: improved decision making generally costs very little but creates enormous shareholder value.

What is true at the top of a company is equally true at other levels. For every decision made by top management, dozens of others are made by middle managers, supervisors, and individual employees. Can you imagine how much better your organization would perform if those lower- and midlevel decisions were better or smarter?

Fortunately, better decisions at all levels are possible when companies do the following:

- Adopt a rational decision process like the one described in this book

- Train appropriate personnel in that process and the tools of decision analysis

- Improve employee understanding and implementation of the process through repeated use

The importance of having good processes is well understood in business. Since the advent of the quality movement in the 1970s, companies around the world have studied their operational processes, improved them, and trained employees in the principles and techniques of process improvement. Thanks to these efforts, the operational side of most businesses is shipshape.

It is much harder to find examples of companies that have attacked decision quality and decision processes with the same zeal— if at all. General Motors, Chevron/Texaco, Johnson & Johnson, and Boeing are among the exceptions in the United States. As David Matheson and Jim Matheson stated in their book *The Smart Organization*, decision making is the next frontier of the quality movement.[1] Once you have an enterprise that knows how to "do things right," you naturally want decisions that will direct people to "do the right things." That completes the circle and makes for a powerful and competitive company.

The GM Experience

General Motors provides an interesting and well-documented case of a large company that has adopted and institutionalized a rigorous decision process.[2] In this case, we can see how a change agent successfully introduced a solid process, earned its acceptance within the management ranks, improved it over a period of years, and made it part of the company's culture.

The change agent in the GM case was Vincent P. Barabba, who had been recruited in 1987 from his post as head of market research at Eastman Kodak. Barabba's experiences at Kodak, and previously at Xerox, had taught him the importance of establishing a free flow of information between the people who develop the information (market researchers) and those who use it (decision makers). He witnessed the mistakes that occur when information is used ineffectively, particularly when people use market information selectively to support business cases for which they advocate. The Kodak experience had also exposed him to the principles of decision analysis.

Beginning in 1988, Barabba and a small staff, with assistance from Strategic Decisions Group, a consulting firm that specializes in decision analysis, began training managers in the dialogue decision process (DDP) described earlier in this book. Their objective was to change the automaker's decision approach from one of advocacy to one of inquiry and learning. Their efforts could not have come at a better time: GM was in serious trouble and faced a number of major decisions.

As described by Barabba in a January 2005 interview for this book, the GM culture at the time was for people to "sell" their proposals to top management.[3] Just as attorneys try to win a case for their clients before a panel of judges, managers would put the best possible face on their proposals. These proposals never acknowledged a downside, and alternative choices were never presented. "The last thing you would do in this environment," said Barabba, "would be to tell management, 'There are actually several other ways to approach this problem.' That just didn't happen."

Between 1988 and 1995, when Barabba passed the baton to new leadership for his GM Strategic Initiatives (GMSI) unit, that internal consulting unit had trained twenty-five hundred managers and executives in DDP and had familiarized them with a set of analytical tools for evaluating alternatives. Many of these individuals now sit on one or more of the permanent or temporary "decision boards" within GM, and they expect the people who come before them with proposals to frame the problem correctly, present alternatives, and evaluate each feasible alternative using the appropriate analytical tools.

Every year the dialogue decision process is applied to more key projects within the company, and each application provides a learning experience for the people involved. Those individuals carry that learning to their next decisions. At the same time, the GMSI unit has matured into an effective support organization with substantial analytical skills. As of 2004, it included twenty-five core professionals and a rotating set of managers representing various functions within the corporation.

Results from the GM case are highly encouraging for any organization that wants to improve. Barabba has observed three significant benefits:

- Key decisions at GM are now handled more rationally; the old approach of "selling" projects is no longer tolerated.

- The time between the initial consideration of a project and its implementation has been cut roughly in half. It takes more time to make the actual decision, because more thought and study go into it. However, the time between the decision and the beginning of implementation has been dramatically reduced because people are not second-guessing decisions or lobbying behind the scenes to change them.

- The use of cross-functional decision teams and boards has improved communication and understanding throughout GM's functional organization. Managers and nonmanagers now collaborate with employees in other units. More important, they are more willing than in the past to think about what's best for the company, and not what's best for their units.

Lessons for Organizational Improvement

The GM example is a single case, but its experience and the literature on organizational change hold a number of lessons for companies that want to make effective decision making part of their DNA. Here are six you can use:

1. Get visible support from the top. If the boss states that your mission is important, others will get the message.

2. Start small and be patient. You cannot train everyone at once, nor change the way people make decisions overnight. Both take time. Use small decision situations to experiment and learn.

3. Focus initially on demonstrating the value of a rational decision process to others. When people see its value, resistance will decrease and you'll get the resources you need to expand.

4. Train people in the use of a common process and a common set of decision tools. Have a few staff experts on hand to help decision teams work through the process and do some of the technical analysis of evaluating alternatives.

5. Don't be a hammer looking for a nail. Apply the process and tools only to appropriate decisions.

6. Practice continual improvement. After every decision, conduct an after-action review and ask, "How could we have done this better?" Then apply what you've learned to the next decision.

Perhaps the most profound lesson on implementation was articulated by Vincent Barabba in his 1995 book, *Meeting of the Minds*. "If you change the way people in a company make decisions," he wrote, "you can change the company's culture for the better"—the ultimate improvement:

> *One of the by-products of the repeated application of the DDP at GM has been a noticeable change in the management culture. There has been an observable shift away from a culture of advocacy and adversarial interactions toward one that is more open and cooperative. This effect was unexpected. Our objective was to change the way decisions were made, not to change the culture. But we have come to understand how intimately the two are linked . . .*

Many corporations make the mistake of altering the organizational chart or of trying to change the corporate culture. In the end, these efforts are expensive, painful, and usually doomed to failure . . . If you want culture change to come about—and to stick—stop fiddling with the organizational chart and start changing the decision making process.[4]

What Leaders Must Do

The adoption and implementation of a rational decision process don't simply happen. Someone with organizational clout, like Vincent Barabba at GM, must lead the way. That person must make the case and must build both support and enthusiasm for it.

Perhaps as important, the leadership of the company must demonstrate its intolerance for any proposal or decision that is made through the old selling or advocacy system. "I have a great idea for expanding our business into the Texas market. It should generate close to $12 million in new annual revenue by the end of the third year. And I'll only need about $300,000 to get the project off the ground. Now here's my plan." When a manager comes to them with a pitch like this, the leadership should push back immediately and insist on something better: "We're glad that you're thinking about ways to increase revenues, but we'd like you to go back and do more homework. Get some other people to help out. The more heads we put around this problem, the better. Specifically, we'd like you to think of several ways to expand our revenues. We shouldn't think of Texas as the only opportunity. If this company is going to make a concerted plan to expand revenues, we'd like some alternatives to choose from."

If senior management gives that type of response to every manager who advocates a plan or a problem solution, people will get the message that selling is not the ticket to getting what they want.

How to Begin

Begin in a unit or operation where senior management and employees would truly welcome a change in how decisions are made.

That might be in your information systems unit, where decisions about the e-commerce Web site or information infrastructure are due to be made. It might be in the area that is responsible for developing and introducing new products and services. A task force assigned to the job of developing a new bonus plan might be another candidate.

Wherever you begin, start small and don't allow it to be driven from the top. These are two of the important lessons from the literature of change management. The likelihood of success is greatest when change is instigated in small, fairly autonomous units. Changing an entire organization at once is much more difficult and less likely to succeed. After change on a smaller scale is accomplished and witnessed by employees in adjacent units, diffusion of the change initiative throughout the organization is much more likely. Change is also more likely if it is motivated and controlled within the units where the process change is being made. Top management support is always important, but canned change initiatives driven and controlled from the CEO's office have a poor record of success.

After people see the beneficial effects of your applications of the decision process, they will be more open to trying it. The leadership should encourage the diffusion of the process to other units.

Get Help If You Need It

Relevant experience is always a plus when you're trying to change business processes. The five-step decision process outlined in this book will be new to most people. The same can usually be said for the tools of decision analysis. This suggests that some professional help in the form of decision training and coaching may be a good investment as you introduce a decision process to your organization.

The quality movement provides a useful analogy. Companies that saw the benefits of quality improvements hired outside trainers to teach quality principles and techniques. Once people learned how to do it, they trained their colleagues.

A number of consulting companies specialize in decision training; they can help you surmount the learning curve much more quickly than you would on your own, and they may steer you clear of pitfalls that could sink your effort.

Encourage Continuous Improvement

Like every other process used by your business—order entry, recruiting, manufacturing, and so forth—decision making is amenable to continual improvement. Individuals and teams can get better at making decisions if they make a conscious effort to learn from each experience. That conscious effort often takes the form of an after-action review:

What were the strong points of our decision analysis?

Where could we have done better?

If we could start over again, what would we do better?

Learning from after-action reviews is then carried forward and applied to the next decision. If this is done systematically, individual decision makers and decision teams will become more effective over time. And that will have a growing positive impact on the business.

But don't limit your thinking to improvement in people skills; consider ways in which the decision process itself can be changed for the better. This might involve the choice of who should participate, your methods for framing the decision and generating alternatives, the tools used in analysis, or the manner in which the final decision will be made. You should make every effort to make the process efficient and effective.

Summing Up

- Improved decisions—by employees at every level—can have a major impact on the value of your business. Even a small improvement can make a big difference.

- To improve decisions throughout the company, you must do three things: adopt a rational decision process, train personnel to use the process and related decision analysis tools, and improve implementation of the process through repeated use.

- The General Motors experience indicates how a rational decision process, like the one offered in this book, can be introduced and gradually expanded within a large organization.

- When you introduce a new decision process, start small and expand the process as it demonstrates its value. Enlist top management support, but localize control and responsibility.

- Encourage continuous improvement.

Useful Implementation Tools

This appendix contains two worksheets you may find useful. Both are adapted from Harvard ManageMentor®, an online product of Harvard Business School Publishing. "The Ten Worst Things That Could Happen List" can be downloaded without charge from the Harvard Business Essentials series Web site: www.elearning.hbsp.org/businesstools. You can freely access this and other worksheets, checklists, and interactive tools found on that site.

1. **Stage–Setting Worksheet (figure A–1)** Use this worksheet to think through how you will approach the decision-making process.

2. **The Ten Worst Things That Could Happen List (figure A-2).** Some managers find it helpful to create and have available a list of the ten worst things that could happen at work and what they would do about them. Use this to record your own list, or have a team or work group develop its list.

Stage-setting worksheet

Use this worksheet to think through how you will approach the decision-making process.

Description of decision

Describe a decision that you and your group needs to make:

Participants

List the names and roles of the people you will include in your decision-making group. Identify key stakeholders, experts, and opponents (individuals who may oppose the decision or block its implementation).

Time

How much time is available to make this decision? Does the decision need to be made by a specific date?

Setting

Where will you meet? (If possible, consider using a location that is different from your usual meeting place.)

Decision-making approach

Which approach will you use to make the decision: consensus, majority vote, qualified consensus, directive leadership, or a combination? (Consider the importance and implications of the decision. You may need to reserve the final decision for yourself.)

How will you make the choice if the group reaches an impasse?

Climate

List some questions you might ask to encourage debate:

1.
2.
3.
4.

Anticipate some positions on the proposed courses of action that are up for decision.

How will you strike a balance between advocacy- and inquiry-based debate?

Source: Harvard ManageMentor® on Making Business Decisions, adapted with permission.

FIGURE A-2

The ten worst things that could happen list

Some managers find it helpful to create and have available a list of the ten worst things that could happen at work and what they would do about them. Use this tool to record your own list or have a team or work group develop their list.

Situation	What I/we would do about it
1.	
2.	
3.	
4.	
5.	
6.	
7.	
8.	
9.	
10.	

Source: Harvard ManageMentor® on Crisis Management, adapted with permission.

Financial Tools
for Evaluating Alternatives

Business decisions are often driven by financial concerns.

Should we continue operating our U.K. distribution center, or should we outsource that activity to a supplier?

How long will it take to recoup our investments in alternatives A and B?

Product A and product B are both attractive alternatives for our company, but how many units must each of them sell before we start making money? Which represents the greatest long-term value and rate of return for our company?

It appears that replacing the heating system in our Chicago headquarters makes economic sense, given projected energy costs. But what if energy costs rise only 5 percent, and not the 10 percent you've projected?

What are the rates of return on the three alternatives you've identified?

This appendix explains tools you can use to answer questions like these by means of the following:

- Return on investment

- Payback period

- Net present value (NPV)

- Internal rate of return (IRR)

- Breakeven analysis

- Sensitivity analysis

Return on Investment (ROI) and Payback Period

Returns from an investment can take the form of cost savings, incremental profit, or appreciation in value. To calculate the net return from an investment, simply subtract the total cost of the investment from the total benefits. To calculate the ROI—the ratio of the net return to the cost of the investment—divide the net dollar amount of the return by the total cost of the investment.

Essentially, ROI is a means of comparing returns on money a company spends internally with returns available elsewhere. Generally speaking, an investment's ROI should be reasonably high—more than the company could expect to get by investing, for example, in government bonds.

Let's suppose that the new $100,000 computer-controlled lathe that you are considering would enable the company to save $18,000 per year over the lifetime of the machine, which is estimated to be seven years. The total savings would thus be $126,000, making a net return of $26,000 ($126,00 − $100,000). Applying the formula—$26,000/$100,000—the ROI for the investment is a very attractive 26 percent.

However, companies also want to know the payback period: how long it will take an investment to pay for itself. We already know that the lathe is expected to save you $18,000 a year. To determine the payback period, divide the total amount of the investment by the annual savings expected. In this case, $100,000/$18,000 = 5.56. In other words, the lathe will pay for itself in 5.56 years. Table B-1 provides a year-by-year illustration.

Note that you will not truly begin to reap the benefits of the investment for more than five years. But what if the life-span estimates are wrong, and the extruder wears out after five years? The invest-

TABLE B-1

Cumulative annual savings

Year	Savings	Cumulative savings
1	$18,000	$18,000
2	$18,000	$36,000
3	$18,000	$54,000
4	$18,000	$72,000
5	$18,000	$90,000
6	$18,000	$108,000
7	$18,000	$126,000

ment now appears to be a loser; the company will not even recoup its initial investment.

As analytical tools, ROI and payback period have several benefits:

- They're easy to convey to upper management.

- They remind everyone that wise expenditures pay off financially.

- They adopt a long-term perspective.

- They help you compare various options.

However, there is a drawback to both methods: they ignore the time value of money. Time value is reflected in more sophisticated financial tools: net present value and internal rate of return.

Net Present Value

Net present value (NPV) was introduced in its simplest form in chapter 5; its treatment is expanded here. This analytical tool can be complicated. Because most calculators and spreadsheet programs can make these calculations for you, we'll dispense with the underlying math.

To begin, let's look at the principle that underlies both methods: the time value of money. In effect, this principle states that a dollar you receive today is worth more than a dollar you will receive in the future. The reason? Even assuming no inflation, the dollar you receive today can be invested to earn a return over the remaining years; the same cannot be said for a dollar received five years from now.

For example, consider $1 received today and another $1 received exactly five years from today. Which is more valuable in your view? If you received $1 today and invested it in a money market account with daily compounding interest at 5 percent per year, that dollar would be worth $1.28 at the end of five years. If you waited five years to collect your $1, you'd be $0.28 behind. Conversely, $1.28 received five years from today (a future value) is the equivalent of $1 received today (a present value) when discounted at 5 percent per year.

This time-value concept can be applied widely in business. For example, in evaluating a new business opportunity, you must analyze the cash flow you expect it to provide at various points in the future. But to perform that analysis, you must devise a method for expressing future dollars in terms of present dollars. That's what net present value and internal rate of return calculations allow you to do.

Let's say that your company expects a new product line of wooden coat racks to start generating $60,000 in annual profit beginning one year from now and continuing for the succeeding five years. The questions for the company can thus be phrased as follows: Given this expected profit stream and the $250,000 up-front cost required to produce it, is a new line of coat racks the most productive way to invest the initial $250,000? Or would you be better off investing it in something else?

A net present value (NPV) calculation begins to answer this question by recognizing that the $300,000 in profit ($60,000 per year over five years) that you expect to receive over five years is not worth $300,000 in present dollars; because of the time value of money, it is worth less than that. That future sum of $300,000 must be discounted before it can be expressed accurately in today's dollars. How much it is discounted depends on the rate of return you could reasonably expect to receive had you chosen to put the initial $250,000 investment into something other than the line of coat racks (but similar in risk) for the same period of time. This rate of return is often called the discount rate. In our example, let's assume a discount rate of 6 percent.

The NPV function on your calculator or spreadsheet takes into consideration your initial investment, your yearly cash flow (in this example, profit), your discount rate, and the number of years over which you will receive cash flows. If the resulting NPV is a positive number and if no other investments are under consideration, the investment should be pursued. In our case, the NPV for the line of coat racks is $2,587, a number that suggests it would be an attractive investment.

But what about an alternative investment your company is considering (and good decisions demand that you consider alternatives)? You are still considering the purchase of the $100,000 computer-controlled lathe described earlier. That investment is forecast to produce cost savings of $18,000 each year for seven years into the future. When discounted at 6 percent, this cash flow stream has an NPV of $456, which is just barely positive. When we compare NPVs for the two investments, we see that both are positive, but the one for the coat racks is greater. If you can afford only one of these investments, you should go with the new line of coat racks and put the new lathe investment on hold.

Here we should emphasize the effect of the discount rate on NPV. Suppose the discount rate were 10 percent instead of 6 percent: in that case, the NPV for the lathe would be −$11,244. The lathe would go from being a modestly attractive investment to being a very poor one.

Notice something else about the NPV calculation for the new line of coat racks: even with a 6 percent discount rate, the NPV is far less optimistic than the rosy 26 percent ROI forecast. The point here is that although it's much more difficult to perform (and explain), the NPV analysis results in more sophisticated, more comprehensive evaluations of investment alternatives.

Internal Rate of Return

The internal rate of return (IRR) is another tool that managers can use in evaluating alternatives. It is defined as the discount rate, the rate at which the NPV of an investment equals zero. Typically, when the IRR of one alternative is greater than the expected return of another, the one with the higher IRR should be undertaken.

What's a reasonable rate of return for a business to expect on an investment? Typically, it's well above what it could get on a risk-free investment, such as a Treasury bond. In many instances, companies will set a hurdle rate: a minimal rate of return that all investments are required to achieve. In such instances, the IRR of the investment under consideration must exceed the hurdle rate in order for the company to go forward with it.

Breakeven Analysis

Breakeven analysis is another method that people use when evaluating alternatives. It is useful when you are considering an investment that will enable you to sell something new or to sell more of something you already make. It indicates how much (or how much more) you must sell in order to pay for the fixed investment—in other words, at what point you will break even. With that information in hand, you can look at market demand and competitors' market shares to determine whether it's realistic to expect to sell that much.

In more precise terms, the breakeven calculation helps you determine the volume level at which the total contribution from a product line or investment equals the total fixed costs of producing it. But before you can perform the calculation, you need to understand the components that go into it: contribution, fixed cost, and variable cost.

Contribution is defined as unit revenue minus variable costs per unit; it's the sum of the money available to contribute to paying fixed costs. Fixed costs are items such as insurance, management salaries, rent, and product development costs—items that stay pretty much the same no matter how many units of a product or service are sold. Variable costs are those expenses that change depending on how many units are produced and sold; examples include labor, utility costs, and raw materials.

With these concepts, we can understand the calculation:

1. Subtract the variable cost per unit from the selling price; this equals the unit contribution.

2. Divide total fixed costs, or the amount of the investment, by the per-unit contribution.

3. The quotient is the breakeven volume, expressed as the number of units that must be sold in order for all fixed costs to be covered.

Let's look again at the proposed computer-controlled lathe. Suppose each item produced by the lathe sells for $75, and the variable cost per unit is $22. Here's the breakeven calculation:

$75 (unit price) – $22 (variable cost per unit)
= $53 (unit contribution)

$100,000 (fixed cost) / $53
= 1,887 units (the breakeven volume)

At this point, you must decide whether the breakeven volume is achievable: Is it realistic to expect to sell 1,887 additional hat racks, and if so, how quickly? Note that this volume must be incremental: because you have been producing this type of product all along and the lathe simply represents a way to improve the production process, the compensating sales volume must be above and beyond current sales volume.

The Harvard Business Essentials Web site has a free interactive software tool you can use to run your own breakeven analyses. It was initially created for the finance module of the Harvard ManageMentor® online publication. To access this tool, just go to www.elearning .hbsp.org/businesstools and look for the tools listed with the book titled *Finance for Managers*. And while you are at the site, check for any other downloads that might be useful to you and your business.

Sensitivity Analysis

Sensitivity analysis is a technique used to assess the financial impact, as measured by net present value (NPV), of changes in key parameters of a decision alternative. You conduct sensitivity analysis by identifying the important uncertainties and then setting up best-case and worst-case scenarios for each. The NPV for these scenarios is then calculated.

For example, in the case of your new line of coat racks, several of the key parameters may be highly uncertain: the number of units that you can sell in a year and the selling price per unit. Any surprises here are bound to have a major impact on the NPV of the new product. In almost all cases, you can model these scenarios in an electronic spreadsheet. This approach makes it easy to run the numbers by simply changing one variable at a time.

Notes

Chapter 2

1. David Matheson and Jim Matheson, *The Smart Organization* (Boston: Harvard Business School Press, 1998).

Chapter 3

1. Alan J. Rowe, *Creative Intelligence* (Upper Saddle River, NJ: Prentice Hall, 2004), 68.

2. J. Edward Russo and Paul J. H. Schoemaker, *Winning Decisions* (New York: Currency, 2001), 24.

3. Jeffrey Pfeffer, *Managing with Power* (Boston: Harvard Business School Press, 1992), 63–64.

Chapter 4

1. David Matheson and Jim Matheson, *The Smart Organization* (Boston: Harvard Business School Press, 1998), 24.

2. G. W. Hill, "Group versus Individual Performance: Are N + 1 Heads Better Than One?" *Psychological Bulletin* 91 (1982): 517–539.

3. Matheson and Matheson, *The Smart Organization*, 42–43.

4. Vincent P. Barabba, *Meeting of the Minds* (Boston: Harvard Business School Press, 1995), 191.

Chapter 5

1. Benjamin Franklin, letter to Joseph Priestley, September 19, 1772. Cited in H. W. Brands, *The First American* (New York: Doubleday, 2000), 457.

2. For a discussion of even swaps, see chapter 9, "Tradeoff," in John S. Hammond III, Ralph L. Keeney, and Howard Raiffa, *Smart Choices: A Practical Guide to Making Better Decisions* (Boston: Harvard Business School Press, 1999), 83–108.

3. Alan J. Rowe and Sue Anne Davis, *Intelligent Information Systems* (New York: Quorum Books, 1996), 24.

Chapter 6

1. For a complete discussion of the catchball technique, see George Labovitz and Victor Rosansky, *The Power of Alignment* (New York: John Wiley & Sons, 1997), 90–92.

Chapter 7

1. David Bovet and Joseph Martha, *Value Nets* (New York: John Wiley & Sons, 2000), 41.

2. Robert G. Cooper, "Stage-Gate Systems: A New Tool for Managing New Products," *Business Horizons* (May–June 1990): 45–54.

3. Alden M. Hayashi, "When to Trust Your Gut," *Harvard Business Review*, February 2001, 60–61.

4. Eric Bonabeau, "Don't Trust Your Gut," *Harvard Business Review*, May 2003, 15.

5. Interview with Kim Wallace by Richard Luecke, January 20, 2005.

Chapter 8

1. John S. Hammond III, Ralph L. Keeney, and Howard Raiffa, *Smart Choices: A Practical Guide to Making Better Decisions* (Boston: Harvard Business School Press, 1999), 191.

2. Dan Lovallo and Daniel Kahneman, "Delusions of Success: How Optimism Undermines Executives' Decisions," *Harvard Business Review*, July 2003, 58.

3. Interview with Vincent P. Barabba by Richard Luecke, January 22, 2005.

4. Mitsuo Fuchida and Masatake Okumiya, *Midway: The Battle That Doomed Japan* (New York: Balantine Books, 1955), 91–92.

5. Scott Plous, *The Psychology of Judgment and Decision Making* (New York: McGraw-Hill, 1993), 226.

6. Ibid., 229.

7. Lovallo and Kahneman, "Delusions of Success," 62.

8. John S. Hammond III, Ralph L. Keeney, and Howard Raiffa, "The Hidden Traps in Decision Making, *Harvard Business Review*, September–October 1998, 52.

9. Joseph Strayer, cited in Theodore S. Hamerow, *Reflections on History and Historians* (Madison: University of Wisconsin Press, 1987), 210.

10. Harry S. Truman, *Memoirs, Volume 2: Years of Trial and Hope* (Garden City, NY: Doubleday & Co., Inc., 1956), 332–333.

11. Richard Neustadt and Ernest May, *Thinking in Time: The Uses of History for Decision Makers* (New York: The Free Press, 1986).

Chapter 9

1. Scott Plous, *The Psychology of Judgment and Decision Making* (New York: McGraw-Hill, 1993), 204.

2. "Solomon Asch Experiment: A Study in Conformity," www.age-of-the-sage.org/psychology/social/asch_conformity.html.

3. Dan Lovallo and Daniel Kahneman, "Delusions of Success: How Optimism Undermines Executives' Decisions," *Harvard Business Review*, July 2003, 60–61.

4. James Surowiecki, *The Wisdom of Crowds* (New York: Doubleday, 2004), 22.

5. Ibid., 10.

Chapter 10

1. David Matheson and Jim Matheson, *The Smart Organization* (Boston: Harvard Business School Press, 1998).

2. Vincent P. Barabba, the executive who instigates the decision process within GM, tells the early part of the story in *Meeting of the Minds* (Boston: Harvard Business School Press, 1995). Up to that point, it was a work in progress. Barabba's book, *Surviving Transformation* (New York: Oxford University Press, 2004), completes the story. You can get a capsule view through an archived Webcast produced by

Strategic Decisions Group in September 2004 (and a downloadable executive summary). That Webcast featured Barabba and his successors at GM, www.sdg.com/home.nsf/sdg/eBriefings--eBriefingArchive.

3. Interview with Vincent P. Barabba by Richard Luecke, January 31, 2005.

4. Barabba, *Meeting of the Minds*, 203–204, 219.

Glossary

ADVOCACY APPROACH In decision making, a mode of behavior in which individuals argue in favor of their positions without considering the needs of other departments or the company as a whole. Advocates typically support their positions with favorable data and assumptions while omitting contrary data.

ANALOGY An inference that if two or more things in a new situation match what we experienced in the past, they will probably match in other respects.

ANCHORING A negotiation tactic that attempts to establish an initial position around which negotiations will take place. In the right circumstances, the first person to put a price on the table establishes a psychological anchor point around which discussion and counteroffers will take place.

CATCHBALL A cross-functional method for improving ideas and promoting buy-in among participants. An initial idea is "tossed" to collaborators for consideration. Whoever "catches" the idea assumes responsibility for understanding it, reflecting on it, and improving it in some way. That person then tosses the improved idea back to the group, where it is again caught and, hopefully, improved still further.

CONFIRMING-EVIDENCE BIAS A common bias that encourages people to seek out evidence that supports their point of view while discounting or dismissing contrary evidence.

CONTEXT The environment of interpersonal relationships and behaviors within which ideas and data will be considered and decisions will be made.

DECISION TRAPS Human biases that cause smart people to make poor choices. These include anchoring, overconfidence, confirming-evidence bias, and false analogies.

EVEN SWAP An alternative that is equal in value to one or more other alternatives in a trade-off.

FRAME A mental window through which we view reality or a particular problem.

GROUPTHINK A mode of thinking that afflicts highly cohesive groups whose members strive for unanimity to the point of overriding a realistic appraisal of alternative courses. People afflicted by groupthink are driven toward a convergent view less by objectivity than by social psychological pressures. In doing so, they inadvertently curtail critical thinking and debate and exclude information that conflicts with the group's view.

HYBRID ALTERNATIVE A new alternative formed from the best features of other choices.

INQUIRY APPROACH In decision making, an open process in which individuals ask probing questions, explore different points of view, and identify a wide range of options, with the goal of reaching a decision that the group creates and owns collectively.

INTELLECTUAL WATCHDOG A decision technique which begins by dividing the decision team into two groups. One group then asked to critique and ask for improvement in the other group's decision.

INTUITION The mental process of assessing situations and forming conclusions without the intervention of factual information or analysis. Many believe that what we call intuition is based on memories, pattern recognition, experience, conditioning, and long-held personal biases.

NET PRESENT VALUE (NPV) The present value of one or more future cash flows minus any initial investment costs.

PAYBACK METHOD A method of financial analysis that calculates how long it will take an investment to pay for itself.

POINT-COUNTERPOINT A process of iterative decision improvement involving two groups. One group proposes a decision and includes its reasoning, supporting information, and key assumptions; that proposal is then presented to the second group, whose job is to identify one or more alternative plans and then present those to the first group. The two groups then debate the proposals until everyone agrees on a decision.

PRESENT VALUE (PV) The monetary value today of a future payment discounted at some annual compound rate.

PRIORITIZATION MATRIX An evaluation method used to compare how well various alternatives achieve an objective. It uses weighted scores to rank each alternative; the alternative with the highest score is most likely your best choice.

REFERENCE CLASS FORECASTING A method that requires forecasters to (1) identify a reference class of analogous past projects, (2) determine the distribution of outcomes for those projects, and (3) place the project being considered at an appropriate point along that distribution.

STAGE GATE SYSTEM An alternating series of development stages and assessment gates that aims for early elimination of losing ideas and faster time to market for potential winners.

SUNK COSTS Investments of time or money that cannot be recovered.

TRADE-OFF TABLE A method for comparing the important attributes of alternatives.

For Further Reading

Articles

Bagley, Constance E. "The Ethical Leader's Decision Tree." *Harvard Business Review,* February 2003. If you spring for optional pollution-control devices at your overseas plant, have you violated your duty to maximize shareholder value? This article provides a framework for exposing conflicts between corporate actions and corporate ethics that can help clarify ethical dilemmas—and potentially head off bad decisions.

Bonabeau, Eric. "Don't Trust Your Gut." *Harvard Business Review,* May 2003. Intuition plays an important role in decision making, but it can be dangerously unreliable in complicated situations. The author describes the dangers of intuition, such as a tendency to favor information that confirms our assumptions, a human need to see analogies in past events, and so forth. He offers a new set of analytical tools you can use to leverage your instincts without being sabotaged by their weaknesses.

Charan, Ram. "Conquering a Culture of Indecision." *Harvard Business Review* OnPoint Enhanced Edition, March 2002. Are the managers in your company unable to make tough decisions when they need to? Author Ram Charan, drawing on a quarter-century of observing organizational behavior, says that the inability to take decisive action is rooted in a company's culture. But, Charan notes, because leaders create a culture of indecisiveness, they can also break it. This article provides guidance for leaders who need to move their organizations from paralysis to action.

Garvin, David A., and Michael A. Roberto. "What You Don't Know About Making Decisions." *Harvard Business Review,* September 2001. Most executives think of decision making as a single event that occurs at a particular point in time. In reality, though, decision making is a process that is vulnerable to power plays, politics, personal nuances, and institutional history. Leaders who recognize this make far better decisions than those who persevere in the fantasy that decisions are events they alone control. That said, some decision-making processes are far more effective than others. Most often, participants use an advocacy process, possibly the least productive way to get things done. They view decision making as a contest, arguing passionately for their preferred solutions, presenting information selectively, withholding relevant conflicting data so that they can make a convincing case, and standing firm against opposition. Much more powerful is an inquiry process, in which people consider a variety of options and work together to discover the best solution. Moving from advocacy to inquiry requires careful attention to three critical factors: fostering constructive, rather than personal, conflict; making sure that all participants know that their viewpoints are given serious consideration even if they are not ultimately accepted; and knowing when to bring deliberations to a close. The authors discuss in detail strategies for moving from an advocacy to an inquiry process, as well as for fostering productive conflict, true consideration, and timely closure. They also offer a framework for assessing the effectiveness of your process while you're still in the middle of it. Decision making lies at the heart of leadership, and it requires a genius for balance: the ability to embrace the divergence that may characterize early discussions and to forge the unity needed for effective implementation.

Gary, Loren. "Cognitive Bias: Systematic Errors in Decision Making." *Harvard Management Update,* April 1998. Managers' ability to take a purely rational approach to decision making is hampered by insufficient information about the problems themselves, the limits of available data, and perceptions that inhibit managers' ability to determine optimal choices. Our judgment is directed by a set of systematic biases, or heuristics. This article discusses the three broad heuristics—the availability heuristic, the representativeness heuristic, and anchoring and adjustment—and identifies the thirteen most common decision-making mistakes managers make.

Hammond, John S. III, Ralph L. Keeney, and Howard Raiffa. "Even Swaps: A Rational Method for Making Trade-Offs." *Harvard Business Review,* March–April 1998. How do you make trade-offs when comparing widely disparate choices? In the past, decision makers have lacked a rational and easy-to-use trade-off methodology. To help fill that gap, the authors have developed a system—which they call "even swaps"—that provides a practical way of making trade-offs among a range of objectives across a range of alternatives. Although the even-swap method will not make complex decisions easy, it provides a reliable mechanism for making trades and a coherent framework in which to make them.

(Note: The even swaps described in this article are also covered in the authors' *Smart Choices,* listed under Books.)

Hammond, John S. III, Ralph L. Keeney, and Howard Raiffa. "The Hidden Traps in Decision Making." *Harvard Business Review* OnPoint Enhanced Edition, November 2000. The human mind is prone to distortions and biases that can undermine even the most well-thought-out decision-making process. This article examines eight psychological traps that are particularly likely to affect the way we make business decisions. The best way to avoid these traps is awareness—forewarned is forearmed. The authors also show executives how to take other simple steps to protect themselves and their organizations from various kinds of mental lapses. (Note: The traps described in this article are also covered in the authors' *Smart Choices,* listed under Books.)

Lovallo, Dan, and Daniel Kahneman. "Delusions of Success: How Optimism Undermines Executives' Decisions." *Harvard Business Review,* July 2003. Three-quarters of business initiatives flounder; new manufacturing plants, mergers, and acquisitions seldom reach their expectations. Why? The answer, according to these authors, is delusional optimism. Businesses overemphasize the potential benefits, underestimate the costs, and ignore the possibility of big mistakes. Lovallo and Kahneman describe key cognitive biases that make executives view the world through rose-colored lenses. Better still, they offer a prescription for what they call the "outside view," which can help decision makers make more realistic assessments of their forecasts.

Morgan, Nick. "Put Your Decision Making to the Test: Communicate." *Harvard Management Communication Letter,* November 2001. Communication is an essential part of good decision making. This article proposes that the process of developing the communications case itself is the single best method for ensuring a good decision. Morgan writes, "If you can tell a convincing story that presents the basis for your decision to a skeptical colleague, explaining what it is and how you arrived at it, what the alternatives were and why you rejected them, then the chances are good that you've given your decision sufficient thought."

Stauffer, David. "How Good Data Leads to Bad Decisions." *Harvard Management Update,* December 2002. Why do many leaders base current decisions on past situations that seem analogous? Because they misremember. Making a decision based on historical precedent has numerous pitfalls, and often you realize too late that the earlier situation was quite different from the current one. Although it's beneficial to use past experiences and decisions, you need to understand how to make the best decisions given today's situation.

Straus, David, and Pat Milton. "Collaborative Decision Making." *Training and Development,* July 2003. Command-and-control decision making is passé, right? But reaching for consensus is not always ideal, especially if time constraints interfere. What's a leader to do? This article outlines a practical framework for determining the appropriate level of stakeholder involvement in a variety of decision-making situations

Books

Hammond, John S. III, Ralph L. Keeney, and Howard Raiffa. *Smart Choices: A Practical Guide to Making Better Decisions.* Boston: Harvard Business School Press, 1999. Making smart choices is a fundamental life skill, relevant to anyone: managers, doctors, lawyers, teachers, students, parents, young, old. Because your decisions shape and influence the course of your professional career and the quality of your personal life, the ability to make good decisions is a key factor in determining whether you achieve your goals. *Smart Choices* blends the art and science of decision making into a straightforward approach for making tough choices. Authors Hammond, Keeney, and Raiffa, among the world's best-known experts on resolving complex decision problems, blend the art and the science of decision making into accessible steps that lead you to consider your choices both intuitively and analytically. Their method can be applied to business, personal, and family decisions.

Mackay, Charles. *Extraordinary Popular Delusions and the Madness of Crowds.* New York: Barnes & Noble Books, 2004. Initially published in 1841, this book contains Mackay's study of crowd psychology, mass mania, and human folly through the ages. These include various swindles, scams, fads, and delusions. Mackay (1814–1889) was a Scots journalist, popular author, and songwriter. His work has generated enduring interest, particularly among investors who follow the "contrarian" form of that art. Anyone interested in decision making will find Mackay's descriptions of flawed human judgment to be both entertaining and instructive.

Matheson, David, and Jim Matheson. *The Smart Organization.* Boston: Harvard Business School Press, 1998. This book identifies the key practices that enable successful organizations to deliver a stream of winning products and services. Smart organizations, say the authors, have internalized nine interlocking principles that are essential in creating corporate cultures that emphasize making the right strategic decisions at the right time. These principles include embracing uncertainty, making disciplined decisions, and fostering a culture of value creation.

Plous, Scott. *The Psychology of Judgment and Decision Making.* New York: McGraw-Hill, 1993. Written by a social psychologist, this book distills the literature of that field as it pertains to decision making and makes it accessible to lay readers. The author examines individual and group behavior, both critical ingredients of business decision making. Particularly interesting is the section "Heuristics and Biases," which includes chapters on probability and risk, anchoring, attribution, correlation, causation, and control.

Rowe, Alan J. *Creative Intelligence*. Upper Saddle River, NJ: Prentice Hall, 2004. Generating feasible alternatives is one of the essential skills of the decision maker. Creativity plays an important part in this skill. In this book, Alan Rowe introduces four types of creativity—intuition, innovations, imagination, and inspiration—and offers strategies you can use to tap in to them.

Rowe, Alan J., and James Boulgarides. *Managerial Decision Making*. New York: Macmillan, 1992. This fine book examines decision making from four perspectives: decision makers and their styles; the organizational context of decision making; creative problem solving and decision tools; and the strategic implications of globalization and environmental change on decision making. Packed with insights and examples from business organizations.

Russo, J. Edward, and Paul J. H. Schoemaker. *Winning Decisions*. New York: Currency, 2001. These authors attack the subject from four angles: framing, gathering intelligence, reaching conclusions, and learning from experience. This last makes it particularly unique and useful. The book contains worksheets and many case examples drawn from the authors' experiences with major corporations.

Surowiecki, James. *The Wisdom of Crowds*. New York: Doubleday, 2004. This intriguing little book by James Surowiecki, a financial writer and regular contributor to *The New Yorker*, states that the collective judgment of many is often smarter than that of one or a few experts, no matter how brilliant. This view is contrary to that held by generations brought up on Mackay's classic, *Popular Delusions and the Madness of Crowds*. Surowiecki cites four conditions under which the many are smarter than the smartest few: there is a diversity of opinion; people's opinions are independent (i.e., not determined by those around them); participants draw on local knowledge; and a mechanism is present for turning private judgments into a collective decision. Examples from science, economics, business, and military history illustrate these points.

Index

About the Subject Adviser

ALAN J. ROWE is a distinguished emeritus professor of management and organization at the University of Southern California. He holds BS and MS degrees in industrial engineering from Columbia University. His dissertation describes one of the first uses of computer simulation for industry.

Dr. Rowe was the director of industrial dynamics on the corporate staff of Hughes Aircraft, where he was responsible for project management systems and for all computer applications. While on the corporate staff of General Electric, he consulted with the 110 operating departments. He was the manager of research at System Development Corporation, where he applied one of the earliest simulation models for management.

He has authored or coauthored twelve books, including *Creative Intelligence, Intelligent Information Systems, Strategic Management: A Methodological Approach*, and *Managerial Decision Making*. In addition to his industry experience, Dr. Rowe served as the chair of the management department and the associate dean and acting dean of the school of business at the University of Southern California. He was president of USC's Phi Kappa Phi honor society and received its Distinguished Member Award. He also received the Pepperdine University Distinguished Diploma of Honor.

His most recent book, *Creative Intelligence*, takes a bold new approach to understanding and applying creativity.

About the Writer

RICHARD LUECKE is the writer of several books in the Harvard Business Essentials series. Based in Salem, Massachusetts, Luecke has authored or developed more than forty books and dozens of articles on a wide range of business subjects. He has an MBA from the University of St. Thomas. He can be reached at richard.luecke@verizon.net.

Harvard Business Review
Paperback Series

The Harvard Business Review Paperback Series offers the best thinking on cutting-edge management ideas from the world's leading thinkers, researchers, and managers. Designed for leaders who believe in the power of ideas to change business, these books will be useful to managers at all levels of experience, but especially senior executives and general managers. In addition, this series is widely used in training and executive development programs.

Books are priced at $19.95 U.S.
Price subject to change.

Title	Product #
Harvard Business Review **Interviews with CEOs**	3294
Harvard Business Review on **Advances in Strategy**	8032
Harvard Business Review on **Appraising Employee Performance**	7685
Harvard Business Review on **Becoming a High Performance Manager**	1296
Harvard Business Review on **Brand Management**	1445
Harvard Business Review on **Breakthrough Leadership**	8059
Harvard Business Review on **Breakthrough Thinking**	181X
Harvard Business Review on **Building Personal and Organizational Resilience**	2721
Harvard Business Review on **Business and the Environment**	2336
Harvard Business Review on **The Business Value of IT**	9121
Harvard Business Review on **Change**	8842
Harvard Business Review on **Compensation**	701X
Harvard Business Review on **Corporate Ethics**	273X
Harvard Business Review on **Corporate Governance**	2379
Harvard Business Review on **Corporate Responsibility**	2748
Harvard Business Review on **Corporate Strategy**	1429
Harvard Business Review on **Crisis Management**	2352
Harvard Business Review on **Culture and Change**	8369
Harvard Business Review on **Customer Relationship Management**	6994

Title	Product #
Harvard Business Review on **Decision Making**	5572
Harvard Business Review on **Developing Leaders**	5003
Harvard Business Review on **Doing Business in China**	6387
Harvard Business Review on **Effective Communication**	1437
Harvard Business Review on **Entrepreneurship**	9105
Harvard Business Review on **Finding and Keeping the Best People**	5564
Harvard Business Review on **Innovation**	6145
Harvard Business Review on **The Innovative Enterprise**	130X
Harvard Business Review on **Knowledge Management**	8818
Harvard Business Review on **Leadership**	8834
Harvard Business Review on **Leadership at the Top**	2756
Harvard Business Review on **Leadership in a Changed World**	5011
Harvard Business Review on **Leading in Turbulent Times**	1806
Harvard Business Review on **Managing Diversity**	7001
Harvard Business Review on **Managing High-Tech Industries**	1828
Harvard Business Review on **Managing People**	9075
Harvard Business Review on **Managing Projects**	6395
Harvard Business Review on **Managing the Value Chain**	2344
Harvard Business Review on **Managing Uncertainty**	9083
Harvard Business Review on **Managing Your Career**	1318
Harvard Business Review on **Marketing**	8040
Harvard Business Review on **Measuring Corporate Performance**	8826
Harvard Business Review on **Mergers and Acquisitions**	5556
Harvard Business Review on **Mind of the Leader**	6409
Harvard Business Review on **Motivating People**	1326
Harvard Business Review on **Negotiation**	2360
Harvard Business Review on **Nonprofits**	9091
Harvard Business Review on **Organizational Learning**	6153
Harvard Business Review on **Strategic Alliances**	1334
Harvard Business Review on **Strategies for Growth**	8850
Harvard Business Review on **Teams That Succeed**	502X
Harvard Business Review on **Turnarounds**	6366
Harvard Business Review on **What Makes a Leader**	6374
Harvard Business Review on **Work and Life Balance**	3286

To order, call 1-800-668-6780, or go online at www.HBSPress.org

Harvard Business Essentials

In the fast-paced world of business today, everyone needs a personal resource—a place to go for advice, coaching, background information, or answers. The Harvard Business Essentials series fits the bill. Concise and straightforward, these books provide highly practical advice for readers at all levels of experience. Whether you are a new manager interested in expanding your skills or an experienced executive looking to stay on top, these solution-oriented books give you the reliable tips and tools you need to improve your performance and get the job done. Harvard Business Essentials titles will quickly become your constant companions and trusted guides.

These books are priced at $19.95 U.S., except as noted.
Price subject to change.

Title	Product #
Harvard Business Essentials: **Negotiation**	1113
Harvard Business Essentials: **Managing Creativity and Innovation**	1121
Harvard Business Essentials: **Managing Change and Transition**	8741
Harvard Business Essentials: **Hiring and Keeping the Best People**	875X
Harvard Business Essentials: **Finance for Managers**	8768
Harvard Business Essentials: **Business Communication**	113X
Harvard Business Essentials: **Manager's Toolkit ($24.95)**	2896
Harvard Business Essentials: **Managing Projects Large and Small**	3213
Harvard Business Essentials: **Creating Teams with an Edge**	290X
Harvard Business Essentials: **Entrepreneur's Toolkit**	4368
Harvard Business Essentials: **Coaching and Mentoring**	435X
Harvard Business Essentials: **Crisis Management**	4376
Harvard Business Essentials: **Time Management**	6336
Harvard Business Essentials: **Power, Influence, and Persuasion**	631X
Harvard Business Essentials: **Strategy**	6328

To order, call 1-800-668-6780, or go online at www.HBSPress.org

The Results-Driven Manager

The Results-Driven Manager series collects timely articles from Harvard Management Update and Harvard Management Communication Letter to help senior to middle managers sharpen their skills, increase their effectiveness, and gain a competitive edge. Presented in a concise, accessible format to save managers valuable time, these books offer authoritative insights and techniques for improving job performance and achieving immediate results.

These books are priced at $14.95 U.S.
Price subject to change.

To order, call 1-800-668-6780, or go online at www.HBSPress.org

How to Order

Harvard Business School Press publications are available worldwide from your local bookseller or online retailer.
You can also call

1-800-668-6780

Our product consultants are available to help you
8:00 a.m.–6:00 p.m., Monday–Friday, Eastern Time.
Outside the U.S. and Canada, call: 617-783-7450
Please call about special discounts for quantities greater than ten.

You can order online at

www.HBSPress.org

Need smart, actionable management advice?

Look no further than your desktop.

Harvard ManageMentor®, a popular online performance support tool from Harvard Business School Publishing, brings how-to guidance and advice to your desktop, ready when you need it, on a host of issues critical to your work. Now available in a PLUS version with audio-enhanced practice exercises.

Heading up a team? Resolving a conflict between employees? Preparing a make-or-break presentation for a client? Setting next year's budget? Harvard ManageMentor delivers practical advice, tips, and tools on over 30 topics right to your desktop–any time, just in time, and just in case you need it. Each topic includes:

1. Core Concepts: essential information in an easy-to-read format

2. Practical tips, tools, checklists, and planning worksheets

3. Interactive practice exercises and audio examples to enhance your learning

Try out two complimentary topics for Harvard ManageMentor® PLUS by going to: **www.eLearning.hbsp.org**

Harvard ManageMentor is available as a full online program with over 30 topics for $195. Selected topics are also available as printed Harvard ManageMentor Business Guides for $14.95 each and on CD-ROM (4 topics each) for only $49.95. For site license and volume discount pricing call 800.795.5200 (outside the U.S. and Canada: 617.783.7888) or visit www.eLearning.hbsp.org.

HARVARD
ManageMentor®
An online resource for
managers in a hurry